PRAISE FOR *YEAR OF T1*

"Virginia Chandler presents a fascinating ....ay ... aragon-legends from many cultures, including real-world sites associated with their lore, supporting a spiritual journey through the year to awaken their energies within. A treat for all who have desired dragons."

—Diana L. Paxson, author of *Essential Asatru*

YEAR OF THE
MAGICKAL
DRAGON

© Virginia Chandler

ABOUT THE AUTHOR

Virginia Chandler (Atlanta, GA) is a seasoned author of three fiction books, including *The Last Dragon of the North* (Double Dragon Publishing, 2015), and has worked with John Matthews on several books focusing on Arthurian lore and legend. She is a former first officer of the national organization Covenant of the Goddess and is active in her local Pagan community.

a SEASONAL JOURNEY *of* MAGICK & RITUAL

YEAR OF THE
MAGICKAL
DRAGON

VIRGINIA CHANDLER
Foreword by John Matthews

LLEWELLYN PUBLICATIONS | WOODBURY, MINNESOTA

FIRST EDITION
First Printing, 2020

Book design by Samantha Penn
Cover design by Shannon McKuhen
Cover illustration by Anne Stokes
Illustration on page 3 by Llewellyn Art Department
Interior illustrations on pages 23, 168 and chapter illustrations by Anne Stokes

Llewellyn Publications is a registered trademark of Llewellyn Worldwide Ltd.

Library of Congress Cataloging-in-Publication Data (Pending)
ISBN: 978-0-7387-6443-6

Llewellyn Worldwide Ltd. does not participate in, endorse, or have any authority or responsibility concerning private business transactions between our authors and the public.

All mail addressed to the author is forwarded but the publisher cannot, unless specifically instructed by the author, give out an address or phone number.

Any internet references contained in this work are current at publication time, but the publisher cannot guarantee that a specific location will continue to be maintained. Please refer to the publisher's website for links to authors' websites and other sources.

Llewellyn Publications
A Division of Llewellyn Worldwide Ltd.
2143 Wooddale Drive
Woodbury, MN 55125-2989
www.llewellyn.com

Printed in the United States of America

OTHER BOOKS BY VIRGINIA CHANDLER

Arthurian Magic

The Northern Band

The Last Dragon of the North

These words are dedicated to
Jormungandr
From chaos, comes creation
V. C. 2019

ACKNOWLEDGMENTS

Quite simply, without the assurances and unwavering support of John Matthews, this book would never have been written. It is a Great Blessing to have such a wise, caring friend and mentor! Our Galactic Conquest continues...

To my wife, Melody, your patience, support, and love is infinite; I am so blessed.

To my spiritual brother, Kevin Sharpton, your love, enthusiasm, and energy is such a gift! You have been thusly dubbed my Dragon Muse!

To Caitlin Matthews, thank you for your patience and kindness with my frequent Celtic myth and Gaelic language queries! Your friendship is a treasure!

To Heather, thank you for believing in my writing and encouraging my (often) crazy ideas!

DISCLAIMER

This book includes the use of and recipes for oil and incenses. A skin test is recommended prior to use of any oil. Place a small amount of the blended oil on the inside of your elbow, cover with a bandage, and check in twenty-four hours. If you experience any soreness, redness, or irritation, do not use the blend.

"None of the animals is so wise as the dragon. His blessing power is not a false one. He can be smaller than small, bigger than big, higher than high, and lower than low."

—*Chinese scholar Lu Dian (AD 1042–1102)*

"In this year terrible portents appeared in Northumbria, and miserably afflicted the inhabitants: these were exceptional flashes of lightning, and fiery dragons were seen flying in the air."

—*Anglo-Saxon Chronicle (Year 793)*

CONTENTS

DRAGON OIL AND INCENSE RECIPES

DISCLAIMER

This book includes the use of and recipes for oil and incenses. A skin test is recommended prior to use of any oil. Place a small amount of the blended oil on the inside of your elbow, cover with a bandage, and check in twenty-four hours. If you experience any soreness, redness, or irritation, do not use the blend.

FOREWORD

For the millions who watched the TV series *Game of Thrones*, one of the high spots—perhaps *the* high spot—must have been the dragons. So lifelike were these that it was hard to believe that such creatures may never have existed. This is, of course, one of the most asked questions amongst those who love myth and legend. Did dragons ever exist, or were they, as some have suggested, a distant memory of prehistoric beasts, whose bones must have been utterly mysterious to our ancestors?

Ultimately, perhaps, it does not matter. The image of the dragon—fiery breath and all—is so deeply ingrained in our subconscious that it has appeared in just about every culture around the world. From the mighty dragon in the epic poem *Beowulf*, to the three-headed Zmey Gorynych of Russian folklore, to the battling dragons of Merlin's vision on Dinas Emrys in Wales, to the countless dragons of Chinese myth (and those who tamed and rode them just as Daenerys Targaryen in *Game of Thrones*), the dragon is ubiquitous. It is as much a part of our inner lives as it could ever have been if it had existed in the outer world.

For this reason alone, it is surprising that no one has recently focused on the magickal properties of the dragon in esoteric practice. Virginia Chandler's book fills this gap—and does it admirably. She gives us a whole year of working with dragons. Filled with lore, drawing upon her wide-ranging experience as a teacher and practitioner of ritual magic, we are guided though a seasonal progression in which we not only get an opportunity to encounter some of these fascinating creatures up close and personal, but to share their deep wisdom, and to learn how they can impact our own inner lives—offering us strength, energy, and power to help us grow. The emphasis is, throughout, on practical experience, and includes everything the individual or group will need to set up a ritual space and to follow the ancient dragon paths around the year. There is much to ponder on along the way, some fine meditations, and a great deal of helpful advice.

In short, this is a book that could become part of a regular cycle of magickal work, and I have no hesitation in recommending it to everyone interested in myth, folklore, and esoteric wisdom. It may or may not change your life (either is possible), but at the end of a year of meetings with dragons, you will have learned much and experienced the virtually limitless energy embodied by these extraordinary creatures.

John Matthews
Oxford, 2019

INTRODUCTION

YEAR OF THE MAGICKAL DRAGON

Dragons: Keepers. Guardians. Initiators. The Eastern world has long seen the dragon as a mighty creature that embodies wisdom, balance, and strength. Yet, the Western world feared the scaly beast. Mighty in size, with scalding breath, the Western dragons were either hunted and slain, or they were simply avoided at all costs. Some even believe that the Western dragon was a physical creature that was hunted to extinction.

As the ages passed, Western society began to adopt the Eastern world's vision of dragons. Rather than only invoking terror, the Western dragon came to be seen as wise and benevolent, albeit still dangerous. The old myths were and are still told, but the lessons from the old myths became different. New tales were crafted, and the new lore depicted dragons as allies to humans as well as embodying the virtues that Western society holds in the highest regard.

Not surprisingly, there are those who sense that dragons have an even deeper and more meaningful purpose, that there is more, something quite mysterious and wonderful, to these magnificent beings. These seekers sense that the tales and the cultural beliefs concerning the dragons act as beacons that can lead to the discovery of how to interact, perhaps how to actually commune, with these beings.

That is how my journey with dragons began; I felt that there was some mystery, some elusive truth, that lay hidden in the dragon stories that I loved so much. I was mesmerized by the mystery of *why* dragons are a planetwide phenomenon; *why* are dragon stories a part of so many cultures? One question led to another, and quite unintentionally, I began a twenty-something-year journey of dragon discovery. What follows in this book is a path based upon my own journey.

What is to be gained by such an endeavor? The seeker certainly needs to examine their motives. Why? Put simply, the path to the dragon's lair is not for the faint of heart. Many dragons not only act as guardians of portals, but *they are* actual portals between worlds. Indeed, and it must be said quite plainly, the domain of the dragon is a perilous place for humans. It *is* a place for potential growth, but growth can be uncomfortable. Simultaneously, though, the change from that spiritual growth can (and hopefully will) allow the seeker to adopt those virtues that the dragons embody.

When this book was first envisioned, its purpose was to act as a tool for the esoteric seeker as they attempt to interact with dragons. As the dragon myths and sacred sites were being explored for use in each chapter, it became quite apparent that there was going to be much, much more than ritual, meditations, stories, and sacred sites for this journey.

As stated before, attempting to commune with the dragons can be a dangerous endeavor. There are very clearly outlined paths to take (and not), words to speak, and gestures to make when dealing with dragons. This book is inspired by and designed to act as a guide for the seeker. It is my intent that this text will give them words to speak and gestures to use for their communion with the dragons.

RITUAL AND MEDITATION

The esoteric path that this book provides follows a basic Neopagan practice of ritual and meditation. The seeker need not be a formally trained magickal practitioner of any sort in order to utilize the material provided. In fact, the first chapter provides a "magickal toolbox" for such things as creating sacred space, making an altar, and making oils for the rituals and meditations that follow in each chapter. The seeker should adopt into their individual (or group) practice whichever settings and tools work best for them.

THE WHEEL OF THE YEAR

The rituals and meditations that follow the first chapter, "Working with Dragon Energy," are designed to coincide with the Pagan Wheel of the Year as it is modernly accepted.

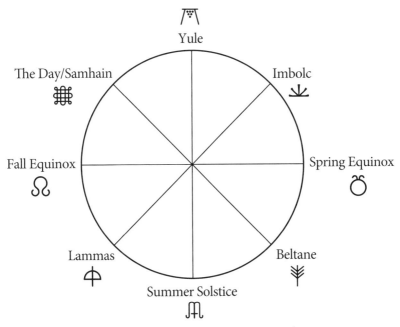

Pagan Wheel of the Year

The Wheel of the Year includes eight sacred days for worship and celebration, which occur about every six weeks. For each sabbat, and in between as well, the seeker will be guided to step into the rhythm of the earth as it travels the annual cycle of the cosmos. Each chapter will focus on a particular position, or sabbat, upon the wheel and will include the dragon energy and dragon lore that corresponds to that particular position upon the wheel.

THE WHEEL WALK

What is a wheel walk? A wheel walk is a spiritual journey wherein the seeker commits a full cycle of the Wheel of the Year focused upon a very specific energy type. Why an entire year? A successful wheel walk displays a commitment that should result in a very strong, energetic bond; the intent is to form a bond forged in trust and love. Indeed, a bond that can and will aid the seeker to grow spiritually.

The seeker is encouraged to follow the wheel walk in the sequence of *your own seasonal setting*. In other words, begin your wheel walk with the book's introduction and chapter one. Then, prepare your chosen sacred space and gather the magickal tools (or not), your choice. Per the calendrical year (and hemisphere!), note where you are in the Wheel of the Year, and then begin the corresponding chapter of dragon magick and lore.

DRAGON LORE

Many of the lessons of dragon kind can be gleaned from the dragon lore, and that is where each chapter will begin. These tales, songs, and poems contain messages from and about dragons that concern much more than tales of heroes and their adventures. Sometimes the message comes directly from the dragon's own voice; at other times, the wisdom within (true to dragon form) is more cleverly hidden.

SACRED SITES

The dragons chosen for this wheel walk all have sacred sites that are very much a part of the dragon lore and the dragon energy with which you will work. Some of these sites are easy to access while others pose greater challenges. Certainly, some of these sites, at least in these modern times, should be avoided, primarily due to human conflicts. However, many of the sacred sites are indeed open and easily reached. The seeker can visit and hopefully even find a private spot to create simple sacred space for a communion with the dragon energy of the site. The descriptions of the sites, even how to arrive at them, are provided in each chapter.

If a physical visit is not an option, then quiet meditations wherein the site is visualized are always an option. Create simple sacred space (see chapter one), and then use your mind's eye to travel to and explore the sacred sites.

DRAGON ARCHETYPES

In my research and communion with dragon energy, I have come to recognize different dragon archetypes. Each archetype has a very specific energy, color, sound, and vibration. Each chapter (and Appendix A) will often refer to these dragon archetypes. As the seeker journeys upon the wheel walk, they will meet many archetypal dragons through story, ritual, and meditation:

Ancestor (Ancient and Mighty Dragons): The oldest and wisest of dragon kind. These dragons were and are co-creators of our world. Their energy penetrates deeply into the earth, runs through every river and ocean, and rides the wind of the vast sky.

Battle Dragons: When there is war in the world of humans, these dragons will manifest and carry the battle into the realms between our world and the world of the gods. The dragon battles of the other planes can (and do!) influence and determine the outcome of conflicts here in our world.

Elemental Dragons: While every dragon possesses all five of the sacred elements, an elemental dragon possesses potent links to a specific element. The dragon's color and vibration are determined by their elemental alignment. We usually refer to these dragons as earth dragons, fire dragons, water dragons, and air dragons.

Guardian Dragons (Sacred Sites and Gods): These dragons are mighty sentinels of very specific locations, objects, and deities. They are loyal and intrepid guardians for sites of worship, thresholds between worlds, relics of power, entrances to the world of the gods, and even for and of the gods themselves.

Primordial Dragons (Chaos and Creation): These dragons were created from or because of the continual cycle of chaos and creation. They actively participate in the cycle as either destroyer/challenger or creator/defender.

Prime Mover Dragons: These dragons have mastered one or more of the five sacred elements and hence are able to move between the worlds with ease. They are essential to the movement of the cosmos; their energy is used to maintain the balance of the universe.

World Dragons: These are the dragons who grasp and hold the tension between all worlds and all things. We know this dragon kind as the ouroboros or world serpent. As long as this dragon remains whole, coiled protectively around all of creation, its tail held within its mouth, then the world is in balance. This dragon symbolizes true wholeness and completeness.

Deity Dragons: Some deities have the power to change their appearance into that of a dragon. These magickal transformations allow the god or goddess to remain in dragon form for long periods of time. Perhaps this dragon form is the "true" form of the gods.

JOURNALING

Recording your experiences as you move along this magickal path will enable you to reflect with more focus. After each meditation, there are suggested journal entries, but the seeker is encouraged to record words, phrases, images, even dreams during the entire Wheel of the Year.

If you already keep a magickal journal, simply add these entries. If you are not a journal keeper, prepare a special notebook and pen, and keep the journal close to you.

CHAPTER ONE

WORKING WITH DRAGON ENERGY

Since dragons can (and do) resonate with all of the elements, including and especially spirit, working with dragon energy requires a very specific practice. Dragon energy is very potent! As many a sage has warned, dragons should *not* be approached lightly.

For the journey ahead, we will be attempting to interact with the energy of dragons. Fortunately for the seeker, the energy of the dragons is all around us. Literally, it is *everywhere*. There are strong lines of electromagnetic energy, sometimes referred to as ley lines, that encircle our planet. These lines are also called dragon lines. Where these lines converge, you will very likely find what is, or once was, a place recognized by humans as a sacred site, such as Stonehenge or the Oracle of Delphi. Many of these sacred sites are also closely linked to dragon lore.

To interact with this dragon energy is to commune with the dragons; if approached wisely, this communion is an amazing and sometimes profound experience. The wisdom needed begins with the seeker being well prepared, and that preparation begins with an understanding of the elements and elementals.

WORKING WITH THE ELEMENTS

Magickal practitioners often work with the elements and elemental energies to construct sacred space. Throughout the course of the upcoming Wheel of the Year, the seeker of dragons is encouraged to use these elements to cast and create magickal circles, to consecrate magickal tools, and to bless sacred space.

The five sacred elements are: earth, fire, water, air, and spirit. Each of the elements has corresponding colors, directions, and symbols. For the purpose of your journey with the dragons, some elemental correspondences are outlined in the table provided.

Element	Earth	Fire	Water	Air	Spirit
Color	Green	Red	Blue	Yellow	Purple
Symbol for casting circle/sacred space	Soil, Salt	Candle, torch	Cup or bowl of water	Incense	Staff, sacred blade, or seeker's hand

Elemental Correspondences

WORKING WITH ELEMENTALS

Our journey will also include working with elemental dragons. While every dragon possesses all five of the sacred elements, an elemental dragon possesses potent links to a specific element. The dragon's color and vibration are determined by their elemental alignment. We usually refer to these dragons as earth dragons, fire dragons, water dragons, and air dragons.

In most Neopagan traditions, the elements are assigned to a particular cardinal direction. However, for this wheel walk, the seeker is encouraged to set up their sacred space per their own geographical location. For instance, if an ocean or lake is right outside your front door and that direction is south, then the seeker is advised to work with the element of water in the southern quadrant of their sacred space. The air element can be welcomed into any cardinal direction as can the earth element. Fire seems to work best when it is set up in the south; but, again, the seeker's sacred space location should determine the elemental correspondences.

It is recommended that the elemental dragons be invited to every dragon communion for their wisdom, power, and protection. Specific calls to the elemental dragons are provided below.

ELEMENTAL CALLS

Air Dragon Invocation

Oh ancient and mighty dragons of air,
Spirits of the guardian dragons,
Watchers of the sacred breath,
I, [practitioner's name], ask you to
Join this sacred space
And lend your wisdom, power, and protection
To [we / I] who do call to you now,
With sacred love and sacred trust.

Fire Dragon Invocation

Oh ancient and mighty dragons of fire,
Spirits of the guardian dragons,
Watchers of the sacred flame,
I, [practitioner's name], ask you to
Join this sacred space
And lend your wisdom, power, and protection
To [we / I] who do call to you now,
With sacred love and sacred trust.

Water Dragon Invocation

Oh ancient and mighty dragons of water,

Spirits of the guardian dragons,

Watchers of the sacred waters,

I, [practitioner's name], ask you to

Join this sacred space

And lend your wisdom, power, and protection

To [we/I] who do call to you now,

With sacred love and sacred trust.

Earth Dragon Invocation

Oh ancient and mighty dragons of earth,

Spirits of the guardian dragons,

Watchers of the sacred earth

I, [practitioner's name], ask you to

Join this sacred space

And lend your wisdom, power, and protection

To [we/I] who do call to you now,

With sacred love and sacred trust.

SACRED SPACE, SACRED TOOLS

With an understanding of the sacred elements in pocket, the seeker is now ready to prepare a physical space and tools (if desired) for communion with the dragons. A vital component of this preparation is designating the space and tools as sacred, or consecrated.

CLEANSING INCENSE

To prepare the space and tools for consecration, a spiritual cleaning is in order. Get a stick of white sage, a small bag of frankincense resin, and a small bag of charcoal disks. (Any local herb or Pagan shop should have these items regularly stocked.) Prepare a cleansing incense by placing about two teaspoons of the frankincense resin in a cup or jar. Add an equal portion of the white sage. Mix the resin and white sage (using a mortar and pestle is fine).

Place a charcoal disk in a heatproof container and light it. Once the charcoal is glowing red, place a pinch of the incense onto the disk.

As the incense is burning, clear and calm your mind. Let any tension flow away from your body. Take a few breaths to wash the cares of the world away. When you feel at peace, take the incense container and walk slowly around your chosen sacred space. Allow the smoke of the incense to fill the space fully; if you walk in a circle, then walk counterclockwise as you cleanse. Visualize any negative energy within this space transforming into positive energy. Place more incense on the charcoal as needed.

When the space has been cleansed, it should feel light(er) and welcoming. If you sense anything that troubles you after the initial cleansing, attempt the cleansing again, just as described above. If the space continues to be unbalanced or just "feel" wrong, perhaps consider another area for your sacred space.

To cleanse any objects that you want to designate as sacred, take the object in hand and use the cleansing incense to "wash" the objects with the smoke. Once the sacred space and tools are cleansed, it's time to consecrate.

CONSECRATION OIL

To consecrate the sacred space and tools, we will use a special oil and chant. To make the consecration oil, you will need:

- 2 tablespoons cleansed frankincense oil
- 7 drops cleansed dragon's blood oil
- 5 drops cleansed patchouli oil
- 3 drops cleansed sandalwood oil
- 1 drop cleansed water
- 3 breaths (yours) upon the mixed oils

Again, any local herb or Pagan shop should have these oils in plenty. After you get the oils, cleanse them using the technique described in the Cleansing section of this chapter.

To declare the water as cleansed, take a bowl or cup, fill it with clean water, and hold the bowl in your left hand. Outstretch your right hand and hold it over the bowl; speak these words:

I declare this water as consecrated to my purpose.

Take the cleansed oils and consecrated water and combine to make the consecration oil. Once the oils and water are combined in a container, hold the container in your left hand. Outstretch your right hand and hold it over the bowl; speak these words:

I declare this oil as consecrated to my purpose.

Pause for three breaths. Then speak the chant:

Hail to the ancient and mighty dragons
Dragons of the sacred breath,
Dragons of sacred flame,
Dragons of the sacred waters,
Dragons of the sacred earth.

With a cleansed space and consecration oil ready, the time has come to construct sacred space.

SIMPLE SACRED SPACE

Each seeker is different, just as each journey is unique; that being said, not all those who seek dragons will want to create a permanent sacred space or facilitate a full-on ritual. That is okay. Still, when communing with the dragons, the seeker should create a sacred spot wherever they may be, whether it's permanent or not. You should take the time to energetically cleanse that spot with incense. This sacred space need only be large enough for comfort and private enough to prevent any disturbances.

If the seeker cannot or prefers not to use cleansing incense to prepare the area, there are other options. Creating a simple sacred space can also be done with quiet thoughts and gentle breathing.

RITUAL SPACE

If you do have the space, indoor or out, that you can dedicate to your communion with the dragons, you are encouraged to do so. Building a magickal dragon temple can be a very rewarding esoteric endeavor. A space that is used only for ritual or meditation can become a very powerful conduit for walking the dragon path.

You will need to identify the cardinal directions of the room or outdoor space and perform a spiritual cleansing first and foremost. If the space has been used for esoteric practice before, it may take multiple cleansing attempts to fully cleanse.

Note: If you are building an outdoor temple, what some call a sacred grove, you will need to take some mundane precautions with your altar and any statuary or other temple items. Wooden altars are lovely, but they will need protection from the elements; similarly, any temple items will need to be sturdy. Otherwise, you are going to be replacing temple items after hard rains, storms, and high winds! There's a high level of commitment to an outdoor temple!

RITUAL ALTAR

Is an altar absolutely necessary to commune with the dragons? In a word, no. But, like a ritual grows in power as it is performed, so, too, will an altar begin to resonate with the dragon energies as it is used. With frequent use and proper tending, your altar will become the focal point for your connection to the dragon energies. Besides, if you are performing the rituals, you will need somewhere to place the ritual items!

As with any altar with an esoteric purpose, a *dragon* altar is a special, sacred object that is reserved for connecting with the dragon spirits. The dragon companions that you will meet on this journey will be your *personal* companions to whom you turn for guidance and wisdom. So, too, will your altar be unique to your experiences and energetic connections to the dragons.

Your altar needs to have a flat surface and be sturdy. Most altars are fashioned from earth-made objects such as wood or stone. The seeker can designate a special piece of furniture or make use of a dresser or desk.

Your altar does not have to be ornate, nor should its creation be driven by dragon "bling." Starting simple is best, and then as your connection to the dragon energies is strengthened, the altar will become more personal and the energy more potent.

CONSECRATING THE ALTAR

Calling the dragon energies to connect with your personal altar can be done with a simple consecration ritual for the altar. The directions, or quarters, upon the altar can be represented with statuary or imagery, which you use to connect to dragons. In short, the seeker can utilize everything mentioned here or nothing at all.

Recommended material for altar: wood or stone

Clearing Incense
- Equal parts of white sage and frankincense resin

Dragon Consecration Oil
- 2 tablespoons consecrated frankincense oil
- 7 drops consecrated dragon's blood oil
- 5 drops consecrated patchouli oil
- 3 drops consecrated sandalwood oil
- 1 drop consecrated water
- 3 breaths (yours) upon the mixed oils

Your consecration preparation will include selecting the location of your altar as well as the altar itself. Cleanse the area chosen for the altar with clearing incense and then do the same to the altar itself. Place the altar in the north. Some magical traditions use the east; it's your choice based on where the element of earth is located. Then, place both of your hands upon the altar. Speak the words:

Here lies the place where the dragon dwells
Here is an entrance to the Cavern of Crystal, Scale, and Stone
Here gather the ancient and mighty dragons of old.

Moisten the index finger of your dominant hand with the dragon conse-cration oil. Place your dominant hand in the eastern quadrant of the altar. Speak the words:

Herein lie the mysteries of the beginning.

Using the oil on your fingertip, draw a symbol of the sun and write the word "Begin" upon the altar.

Moisten the index finger of your dominant hand again with the dragon consecration oil. Place your dominant hand in the southern quadrant of the altar. Speak the words:

Herein lie the mysteries of the mind.

Using the oil on your fingertip, draw a symbol for thought or memory, such as an eye or raven, and the word "Remember."

Moisten the index finger of your dominant hand again with the dragon consecration oil. Place your dominant hand in the western quadrant of the altar. Speak the words:

Herein lie the mysteries of the heart.

Using the oil on your fingertip, draw a symbol for passion or love, such as a heart, and the word "love."

Moisten the index finger of your dominant hand again with the dragon consecration oil. Place your dominant hand in the northern quadrant of the altar. Speak the words:

Herein lie the mysteries of the soul.

Using the oil on your fingertip, draw a symbol for the goddess or earth and the word "Mother."

Speak the words:

This altar is now consecrated as a path to the dragon cavern.
I ask the dragons, ancient and mighty spirits, to bless this
space with their wisdom, power, and protection.
So be it.

EMPOWERING THE SACRED SPACE

To strengthen your communion with the dragon spirits, each quarter of your altar or circle space can also be consecrated to a specific elemental dragon.

For the elemental dragon spirits of air, an air-based symbol on or near the altar can be used. For instance, my personal dragon practice uses a katana sword with a dragon carved into the pommel to represent the air energy. This sword is sheathed and rests against the corresponding side of the altar. Whichever symbol calls to you, touch it after moistening the index finger of your dominant hand with the dragon consecration oil. Speak the words:

Here is a key to the mysteries of the beginning.

To strengthen your bond with the elemental dragons of fire, a fire-based symbol on or near the altar can be used. I use a spear with engraved runes to represent the fire energy. The spear is usually in front of the altar with the spear tip down. Again, whichever symbol calls to you, touch it after moistening the index finger of your dominant hand with dragon consecration oil. Speak the words:

Here is a key to the mysteries of the mind.

To strengthen your communion with the elemental dragons of water, use a water-based symbol on or near the altar. I use a chalice; in fact, I have four chalices that I rotate with each changing season. The chalice represents emotion, healing, and intuition. Whatever symbol calls to you, touch it after moistening the index finger of your dominant hand with the dragon consecration oil. Speak the words:

Here is a key to the mysteries of the heart.

To strengthen your relationship with the elemental dragons of the earth, use an earth-based symbol for the altar. I use a black onyx stone for earth. Whatever symbol calls to you, touch it after moistening the index finger of your dominant hand with the dragon consecration oil. Speak the words:

Here is a key to the mysteries of the soul.

CONSECRATING THE TEMPLE

Indoors or out, the temple consecration is the same. First, consecrate the altar as described earlier in this chapter. Then, you will walk to each quarter and dedicate that quadrant to the appropriate elemental dragon:

Air: Visualize your air altar symbol as you face the quadrant that you have chosen for air. Speak these words:

Here is a gateway to the mysteries of the beginning.

Fire: Visualize your fire altar symbol as you face the quadrant that you have chosen for fire. Speak these words:

Here is a gateway to the mysteries of the mind.

Water: Visualize your water altar symbol as you face the quadrant that you have chosen for water. Speak these words:

Here is a gateway to the mysteries of the heart.

Earth: Visualize your earth altar symbol as you face the quadrant that you have chosen for earth. Speak these words:

Here is a gateway to the mysteries of the soul.

Back at the altar, raise your arms and speak:

Here lies a place where the dragon dwells.
Here is an entrance to the Cavern of Crystal, Scales, and Stone.
Here gather the ancient and mighty dragons of old.
We call upon the mighty dragons.
We dedicate this space to be the crossroads wherein we may meet.
This is the sacred ground, the gateway, the threshold
to the Cavern of Crystal, Scales, and Stone.
May our communion be strengthened.
May your wisdom come to those who seek it.
May the mysteries be revealed to those who wish to see.

PREPARING FOR RITUAL

The rituals included in this guide are designed to take place inside of a magickal circle that has been cast using the five elements. The accomplished ritualist is encouraged to adapt their own casting technique with the recommendations here. For the seeker who is new to ritual, a casting technique is provided.

All of the rituals in this book will cast the sacred circle using clockwise, or deosil, as the direction for the casting of the elements and invitation, or call, to the elemental dragons. The rituals are also written to be accessible to either the solitary practitioner or the coordinated efforts of a working magickal clan. Thus, the [I/we] notations are included in the spoken parts of the workings.

Incense: Each ritual has its own incense recipe that will be listed at the beginning of each sabbat ritual.

Oil: Each ritual has its own oil recipe that will be listed at the beginning of each sabbat ritual.

Altar Candles: Three candles will be used to build dragon ritual space. A purple candle will represent the spirit dragon. Appropriate colors and symbols for the other two candles will be noted for each ritual.

Quarter Candles: Each direction or quarter of the circle can utilize a candle to call the elemental dragons: use green for earth, red for fire, blue for water, and yellow for air.

Chime or **Bell:** As the elemental dragons are called, a bell or chime can be rung as part of the call.

Building a Ritual Fire: In the center of the sacred space, a proper fire should be built either before or as part of the communion with the dragons. Cleanse and consecrate the fire pit with dragon consecration oil (or wherever you will build your fire) before first use. If building a fire is not an option, a candle can be substituted.

Fire Safety: Remember to always have a fire extinguisher or other fire deterrent near the fire! Always practice basic fire safety!

All of the above items should be cleansed and consecrated before use with the dragons. Similarly, once these items are dedicated, they should be stored carefully and only used for working with dragon energy.

CASTING A DRAGON CIRCLE

Each of the rituals in this guide should begin with the creation of a magickal circle. The first step in creating this circle is the casting of the sacred elements.

Start in the earth quadrant of your space. Take a physical representation of the earth element (sand or salt) and walk clockwise around the entire circle of sacred space while casting the element using your dominant hand. In your mind's eye, envision a green earth dragon awakening and joining your sacred space. When you have returned to the earth quadrant, bow and return to your altar.

Take a physical representation (candle or torch) of the fire element and walk to the fire quarter of your sacred space. Walk clockwise around the entire circle of sacred space while casting the element using your dominant hand. In your mind's eye, envision a red fire dragon awakening and joining your sacred space. When you have returned to the fire quadrant, bow and return to your altar.

Take a physical representation of the water element and walk to the water quarter of your sacred space. Walk clockwise around the entire circle of sacred space while casting the element using your dominant hand. In your mind's eye, envision a blue water dragon awakening and joining your sacred space. When you have returned to the water quadrant, bow and return to your altar.

Take a physical representation of the air element and walk to the air quarter of your sacred space. Walk clockwise around the entire circle of sacred space while casting the element using your dominant hand. In your mind's eye, envision a yellow air dragon awakening and joining your sacred space. When you have returned to the air quadrant, bow and return to your altar.

Now, beginning at the altar, bow and walk clockwise around the entire circle of sacred space. In your mind's eye, envision a purple spirit dragon awakening and joining your sacred space. When you have returned to the altar, bow.

CALLING THE ELEMENTAL DRAGONS

After the elements have been cast, you should invite the elemental dragons to join your space. Stand in the earth quadrant and speak the words of the earth dragon call:

[If using a quarter candle, light it now]

Earth Dragon Invocation

Oh ancient and mighty dragons of earth,
Spirits of the guardian dragons,
Watchers of the sacred earth,
I, [practitioner's name], ask you to
Join this sacred space
And lend your wisdom, power, and protection
To [we/I] who do call to you now,
With sacred love and sacred trust.

[If using a chime or bell, ring it now]
[bow]

The fire dragons are called next. Walk to the fire quadrant of your space and speak the fire dragon call: [If using a quarter candle, light it now]

Fire Dragon Invocation

Oh ancient and mighty dragons of fire,
Spirits of the guardian dragons,
Watchers of the sacred flame,
I, [practitioner's name], ask you to
Join this sacred space
And lend your wisdom, power, and protection
To [we/I] who do call to you now,
With sacred love and sacred trust.

[If using a chime or bell, ring it now]
[bow]
The water dragons are called next. Walk to the water quadrant of your space and speak the water dragon call: [If using a quarter candle, light it now]

Water Dragon Invocation

Oh ancient and mighty dragons of water,
Spirits of the guardian dragons,
Watchers of the sacred waters.
I, [practitioner's name], ask you to
Join this sacred space
And lend your wisdom, power, and protection
To [we/I] who do call to you now,
With sacred love and sacred trust.

[If using a chime or bell, ring it now]
[bow]
The air dragons are called next. Walk to the air quadrant of your space and speak the air dragon call: [If using a quarter candle, light it now]

Air Dragon Invocation

Oh ancient and mighty dragons of air,

Spirits of the guardian dragons,

Watchers of the sacred breath,

I, [practitioner's name], ask you to

Join this sacred space

And lend your wisdom, power, and protection

To [we / I] who do call to you now,

With sacred love and sacred trust.

[bow]

THE WORLD DRAGON, JORMUNGANDR

To begin the wheel walk with the dragons, we will first visit the dragon lore and lessons of a Norse world dragon, Jormungandr.

Jormungandr is a Midgard sea serpent, but he is not confined to the element of water. The water *is* where he dwells and from which he emerges, but he has the power, knowledge, and wisdom of all the elements: his scales are as hard as the mountains, his venom scalds like fire, the water is his domain and, when he emerges from the sea, his body fills the sky.

As Jormungandr grew within the depths of the sea, he became enormous and was able to encircle the entire world with his body. Once he had all of Midgard surrounded, he took his tail into his mouth, and thus he became infinity.

While he rests and is at peace, he is the serpent eating his own tail. In this position, Jormungandr is the Norse flavor of the ouroboros. Like the shared sacred sites mentioned earlier, the ouroboros has been depicted by many cultures; and, insofar as we can tell, they all appear to symbolize wholeness. The earliest depiction of this symbol is from an Egyptian funerary text which is about Osiris and his underworld meeting with the god, Ra. The ouroboros is shown twice on the figure and most experts believe this to be a symbol of the beginning and ending of time, or, infinity.[1]

---

1. Ra Un Nefer Amen, *Metu Neter, vol 1: The Great Oracle of Tehuti and the Egyptian System of Spiritual Cultivation* (New York: Kamit Publications, 1990), 97.

The phrase "the all is one" is also a part of the energy of the world serpent. It is and represents the journey to wholeness of both the seeker's personal quest and the creation (from chaos) of the world.

Jormungandr, the Norse World Serpent

THE SEEKER'S WORLD JOURNEY

The Norse tale of Ragnar Lothbrok and his "winning" of the daughter of the Geatish king Harold is an example of how an individual's journey can parallel the ouroboros. In this tale, Thora Borgarhjort, Harold's daughter, is gifted with a small lindworm, or dragon, by her father. The dragon grows and encircles the child's crib and then takes its own tail into its mouth; the child's world is complete and in balance.[2]

Along comes Ragnar, who must slay the dragon in order to win Thora's hand in marriage. Ragnar, like many heroes before and since, "slays" the serpent and emerges victorious from the encounter. Ragnar's journey brings chaos upon Thora's personal world but the chaos is necessary for the two of them, Ragnar and Thora, to become the tools themselves of creation.[3]

---

2. Ben Waggoner, trans., *The Sagas of Ragnar Lodbrok* (Chicago: The troth Publications, 2018), 4.

3. Waggoner, *The Sagas of Ragnar Lodbrok*, 4–6.

Likewise, the ouroboros, the world dragon, is born from chaos and from that chaos, comes destruction and then rebirth. Just as Jormungandr will unleash Ragnarok when he releases his tail, it will also signal the beginning of a new cycle of energy, and the slain gods will rise again. The tale will continue. The world serpent will grow and encircle the world, bringing wholeness out of nothing.

MEETING A GUARDIAN DRAGON THROUGH MEDITATION

And now it is time to begin the Journey. Go to your sacred space or create a simple sacred space. Clear your mind and let the mundane world's troubles and cares rest aside for this time.

If you are experiencing this meditation alone, record the meditation or have someone you trust read it to you during this communion with the dragons.

Whether alone or with a group during ritual, perform this meditation in your sacred space. Ensure that your surroundings are quiet and that you are completely comfortable (temperature, clothing choice, sitting or lying down, etc.). Make sure that this experience will not be spoiled by mundane annoyances!

Close your eyes and breathe deeply. Allow the cares and concerns of the mundane world to roll away from your neck … your shoulders … your arms … your fingers. Allow your back to relax, from your neck down, down, down, to the base of your spine … and just breathe ….

Allow your focus to rest behind your closed eyes as you feel your body relax completely. You are still. You are quiet.

In your mind's eye, see yourself on a rocky hillside. There are scatterings of dew-moistened grass, but there is more rock than green. The air is clear and fresh. The sun is warm upon your face. The energy of this place, of this time, is solid, good, and strong.

You stand at the bottom slope of a tall, snow-crested mountain. As you look up, you see a path that leads up the mountain, but the way is not clear, and your eyes quickly lose the path in a grey haze.

The haze appears to be fog, or perhaps clouds. In the distance, you can hear the crashing of waves and you immediately smell the brine of the sea. The air is damp but not chilled, and it looks as if the fog is clearing just ahead of you.

Begin walking upon the mountain path, slowly, slowly, slowly ascending. Each footstep is deliberate and sure. Your breathing is deep and satisfying.

The mountain shakes and rumbles, causing you to pause. Above you, storm clouds gather. You feel the need to find shelter until the storm passes.

Take a few more steps and you will see a stone to the left of the path. Upon the stone you see runes and the unmistakable image of a coiled dragon.

Look more closely at the stone. Focus on the runes. Around your shoulder, you are wearing a small satchel. Reach into the satchel and you will find a leather-bound journal and a writing stylus. Draw the runes that you see on the stone. If are unable to see the runes at this time, try to focus on just one. If the runes are still not revealed, all is well as you can return to this place at any time.

There is a little-used path leading from the stone. Take that path. Within a few steps, you see an opening in the mountain, a cavern. The entrance is just your height and wide enough for you to easily enter, but you cannot see anything beyond. The darkness beyond is complete.

Look to the right of the cavern's entrance. There you will find a torch, lantern, or candle. Take the light and step into the cavern.

As soon as you are inside, your light ignites, and the cavern is revealed to you.

Take a few moments to inspect the cavern. Look first at the floor. Is it stone? What color? Sand or dirt? How does the cavern smell? Is the air damp or dry? Is there water anywhere nearby that you can see or hear?

Take three deep breaths.

Look at the cavern's walls. What color are they? Are they stone? Are there drawings?

Take three deep breaths.

Sit down in the cavern and close your eyes. You hear a distant voice. In your mind's eye of your mind's eye, you see a dragon … a green earth dragon that may appear to you as winged or as serpentine. She is far away … but she is coming closer.

This is the entrance to the Cavern of Crystal, Scale, and Stone.
I am its guardian. Speak your name and declare why you have come.

Bow your head as you send your name silently to the guardian. Tell the guardian that you wish to build your communion with the dragons. That you wish to learn from their wisdom.

Remove your shoes and sit in the center quietly.
You are welcome here. You now know the path to this place and
will find it easily. Do not venture elsewhere until I have shown you!
You must prove trustworthy, and your heart must prove true.
You will be watched, Seeker, for that is what we shall call you,
for now: "Seeker." Go now and remember!

Take three more deep breaths. Concentrate upon the back of your closed eyes. With your next breath, you feel a shift in the energy around you. You begin to feel a bit heavier as you become aware of your body.

When you open your eyes, you will have returned to your safe and sacred space in this world. You will feel refreshed by this communion with the dragons.

Now, one more deep breath … and open your eyes.

JOURNAL ENTRIES

1. Record the runes, or whatever you saw, such as symbols, upon the stone which leads to the Cavern of Crystal, Scale, and Stone.

2. What type of lighting device did you use to light the cavern? Record it in your journal.

3. Describe your vision of the green guardian dragon.

THE WHEEL TURNS

Now that you have met a guardian dragon, take some time to reflect upon that experience. You have truly begun an exciting journey with the dragons! Continue to spend quiet time in your sacred space and reflect upon what you hope to experience and gain from this wheel walk. If you wish, conduct the meditation again and use your journal to document each visit to the cavern as well as any insights that may come to you.

As you prepare to study and meet the dragons that are included in this guide, remember to be patient; this wheel walk is intended to be slow and steady. First, note where you are in the seasonal calendar. Is it spring? Winter? Fall? Here is a celestial event chart with the sabbat and chapter correspondences for your wheel walk. Find where you are in this chart and continue your wheel walk with the corresponding chapter.

Celestial Event	Sabbat	Chapter
Fall Equinox: balance between night and day	Autumnal Equinox	Chapter 9 Harvest Dragons
Exact midpoint between Autumnal Equinox and Winter Solstice	Samhain	Chapter 2 Ancestor Dragons
Winter Solstice: shortest day of the year	Yule	Chapter 3 Ice Dragons
Exact midpoint between Winter Solstice and Spring Equinox	Imbolc	Chapter 4 Hearth Dragons
Spring Equinox: balance between night and day	Vernal Equinox	Chapter 5 Waking Dragons
Exact midpoint between Spring Equinox and Summer Solstice	Beltane	Chapter 6 Dragons of Making
Summer Solstice: longest day of the year	Litha	Chapter 7 Golden Dragons of Summer
Exact midpoint between Summer Solstice and Autumn Equinox	Lughnasadh	Chapter 8 Dragons of Victory

Celestial, Sabbat, and Corresponding Chapter Chart

CHAPTER TWO

SAMHAIN AND THE ANCESTOR DRAGONS

The word "Samhain" is Gaelic and originated from the Gaelic words *samain*; *sam*, which means "summer," and *fuin*, which means "end." Quite literally, Samhain means "summer's end." The early British cultures believed that the year was divided in half: a dark half and the light half. Samhain marked the end of the light half and the beginning of the Celtic new year, or the dark half.

Samhain finds the seeker at the exact midpoint between the Autumn Equinox and the Winter Solstice. In the Wheel of the Year, this is the final harvest celebration. Physically, the earth has yielded all of her gifts from the growing season. Preparation for winter begins with the gathering of these last crops along with ensuring that the seeker has proper shelter from the coming cold. An important part of this celebration is giving thanks for what the earth has yielded so that we may live.

Samhain is also very closely tied to our ancestors. It is believed that at this point upon the wheel, the portals between all of the worlds are very thin. Communicating with our ancestors is more easily accomplished. For this reason, honoring our ancestors is also very frequently practiced during this sabbat.

For this portion of the wheel walk, the ancestor dragons will be honored. Let us go back, then, to the oldest of dragons, those that were there at the great beginning. These old dragons have much to teach, and many lessons can be learned. We will use their stories, first and foremost, to familiarize the seeker with the dragon. Then, the teachings of the dragon will be highlighted. Finally, using sacred space, the ancestor dragons will be approached and honored.

LORE OF THE ANCESTOR DRAGONS

Tiamat of Babylonia

One of the most ancient of dragons is the Babylonian goddess Tiamat. According to her descriptions in the ancient texts, Tiamat appeared as both human and dragon. She is one of the Annunaki, the old gods, and is called *Ummu – Hubur*, "she who formed all things." Yet, she is far from a gentle Mother creator goddess. During the time of creation, Tiamat shone with sea water as she roared and smashed the world into existence. With her partner, Abzu, she filled the emptiness of the world with the waters needed for the cycle of life to begin. It was beautiful *and* violent.

The wisdom from Tiamat's lore teaches us that primeval chaos is fierce and dangerous. The wise seeker will heed this wisdom with every step upon the journey. Tiamat teaches us that change is rarely comfortable, and for big change, one can certainly expect major discomfort. Yet, Tiamat also brought forth the *world* through chaos and violence. From chaos comes creation.

Mushhushshu-dragon, Dragon of Marduk

The Mushhushshu-dragon, or "striding dragon," is also known as the "dragon of Marduk." Marduk is one of the oldest gods of Mesopotamia and was the patron god of ancient Babylon. It was Marduk who challenged the great Tiamat, the dragon goddess of the primordial sea, and slew her. It was Tiamat's remains that formed the first lands.

Marduk's dragon is depicted on Babylonian cylinder seals and, most famously, on the Gate of Ishtar. This ancient dragon is a creature with scales covering its body, a serpentine head with viper horns, the front feet of a cat, the hind legs of a bird, and a tail much like a scorpion's. On the Babylonian cylinder seals, the Mushhushshu-dragon rests near Marduk's feet, its eye wide open and tongue protruding. The horns resemble a crown of sorts, and the dragon seems ever watchful and aware.

One of the many lessons from Marduk's dragon concerns spiritual transformation. This lesson is perhaps best exemplified in the ancient annual celebration in Babylonia where the worshippers would walk what was called the Processional Way.

The Mushhushshu-dragon, Marduk's dragon, adorned the sacred Gate of Ishtar. This gate was the beginning point for the annual procession of priests and worshippers that led to the Temple of Marduk, which rested atop a ziggurat at the end of the Processional Way. The Processional Way was a half mile long with walls of over fifty feet on each side. Of course, to take part in the sacred journey, the participants had to first pass through the Gate of Ishtar.

The Gate of Ishtar was a threshold of transformation; by walking through it, the seeker signaled to the gods that they were eager and willing to traverse the path which led to the sacred space of the mighty god Marduk. The gate itself was dedicated to the goddess Ishtar, although her sacred animal, the lion, is not found on the front of the gate. Instead, the front panel of the gate has alternating images of the Mushhushshu-dragon and a bull, the bull being the sacred animal of the god Adad.

The Mushhushshu-dragon itself is a guardian of the sacred way; it is a protector and companion of a god and his sacred space. One of this dragon's lessons is that for the seeker to approach and commune with the gods, one must first traverse a threshold that will be guarded closely by these magnificent creatures.

Kur of Sumeria

In ancient Sumeria, we find perhaps the oldest dragon slaying tale, the tale of Kur and Enki. In the metaphysical sense, the "slaying" of a dragon signals the alchemical transformation of both dragon and slayer. Many times, the transformation will echo and affect the entire world. Most certainly, these echoes can also transform us.

In this tale, the hero Enki goes to slay the dragon, Kur, in order to rescue the goddess, Ereshkigal. Enki must descend into the Netherworld and does so in a boat. The references to the elements and how the hero and dragon must both traverse them is critical to gleaning the wisdom from this particular dragon-slaying story: Kur attacks the hero with a flurry of stones (an earth element) of all sizes. This dragon can (and does) hurl boulders, pebbles, and hailstones. He also uses the dark and swirling waters of the Netherworld to attack the bottom of Enki's boat. The dragon thus utilizes the earth and water to defend itself, showing mastery over both elements.

Then, the tale goes completely silent. The tablets upon which the remainder of the tale is inscribed are missing, most likely broken away. Yet, the silence from the missing text can still be seen as a part of the journey that can lead to an even deeper understanding of the tale. For instance, in ancient Sumer, Kur was also the name for the entire underworld. From this perspective, the dragon itself is a deep, open cavern that is a shadow world of our own. Kur, the dragon, is a dense, thick manifestation who is a guardian of the underworld. His message of wisdom for us, at least for now, is to be silent. To watch. To defend.

Illuyankas of Hattusa

In the ancient world of the Hittites, the storm god, Taru, and the dragon Illuyankas were mortal enemies. Their battle was reenacted every spring by the Hittites as part of *puruli*, their spring festival. The *puruli* festival was a celebration and blessing for the well-being of the people and for the fertility of the land.

Illuyankas was a chaos dragon, and he fulfilled his duties as such rather well. This dragon was able to defeat the storm god during their first battle and came very close to slaying the god, which threatened the entire cycle of existence.

The balance had to be re-established, so Taru sought the wisdom of the other gods. It was Inara, goddess of wild animals and Taru's daughter, who devised the plan and the means to end the dragon's chaotic supremacy over the land.

Inara becomes the lover of a mortal man in order to gain the "trick" that will destroy the dragon and end the chaos. Her lover advises the goddess to host a great festival and lure the dragon (and his family) to attend. There, they will encourage the dragon to gorge himself on food and drink. Once the dragon is intoxicated and weakened, he can be bound and destroyed. The plan is successful: Taru and the other gods wait until Illuyankas is quite drunk and then bind him with ropes. Taru swiftly kills him.

We will see this luring of a dragon to something that he or she desires, whether it be food, drink, or treasure, in other tales. The "dragon slayer" and dragon are, each and every time, transformed. Balance is restored. The land and the people rejoice.

Yam: Nahar of the Seven Heads

From the dragon lore of the land of Canaan comes still another ancient chaos dragon, Yam-Nahar of the Seven Heads. Like Tiamat, Yam-Nahar is primordial destruction (and creation); he is a sea dragon with power that is untamed and raging. Initially, he is gifted lordship over the other gods by their father, El. Yet, his rule becomes oppressive, and the other gods want to be rid of him. It is the goddess Asherah, consort of El, who takes action when their pleas go unheard by the tyrannical Yam-Nahar: she offers to become his lover.

Baal, one of the chief gods, is outraged that Yam-Nahar accepts their mother's sacrifice; he vows to end the madness and restore balance to the world. Baal receives a set of magical weapons from the craftsman Kothar-wa-Khasis and declares that he will slay the great dragon.

A magnificent battle ensues atop a great mountain; when it is done, Baal is victorious. Yam-Nahar is defeated and thus order is restored. For the world and its people, the cycle of chaos and order begins anew.

Mehen, Cosmic Serpent, Protector of Ra

Even the gods need protection (as we have seen) and the great Ra of Egypt is no different. Every day as Ra travels the sky, Mehen coils around the god's Sun Boat and guards against any threat to Ra's task. His name, Mehen, actually means "coiled one" in Egyptian. This dragon was well known to the ancient Egyptians; they recognized how important it was for every facet of the daily sun cycle to operate exactly as intended.

While Mehen's adversary, Apep, was shunned and actively banished by the Egyptian people, Mehen was very much appreciated for his role in the cycle of day and night. In fact, many game boards have been found in burials that are clearly tied to Mehen; the game was called "Mehen" or "Game of the Snake." The game boards are circular and are actually formed into the shape of a coiled serpent. The head of Mehen was often included on the board and usually lay near the center while the tail was carved into the outer ring.

Unfortunately, we do not (yet) know precisely how the game was played; we do know that there were marbles and animal figurines involved. The playing squares of the board, which are part of the coiled Mehen, we think were used for movement on the board. Even today, we do not know if this board was purely recreational or perhaps held some mystical influence or connection with Mehen or Ra. Perhaps it was both.

Apep, Serpent of the Nile (also called Apophis)

Also from the land of Egypt, we find the energetic opposite of Mehen: this Egyptian dragon is known as the *Enemy of Ra, Lord of Chaos;* it is the giant serpent called Apep. This chaos dragon is the cyclic adversary of the solar deity, Ra, and Ra's companion, Mehen. Akin to the lore of our other ancient and mighty chaos dragons, the two deities battle, and through their actions, the world is kept in balance. Daily prayers were offered by the priests to aid Ra in this battle; in fact, the priests composed a very detailed guide for how to ensure that Apep never conquered Ra. The writings are called *The Book of Overthrowing Apep*, and for the first time, we have a step-by-step guide for how to hold the chaos at bay. The spells include:

Spitting Upon Apep

Defiling Apep with the Left Foot

Taking a Lance to Smite Apep

Fettering Apep

Taking a Knife to Smite Apep

Putting Fire Upon Apep[4]

Yes, indeed, Apep is the Egyptian ouroboros.

SACRED SITES OF THE ANCIENT
AND MIGHTY DRAGONS

Ancient Babylonia and Sumeria, Modern-Day Iraq

Dragon seekers may find that travelling to the lands of ancient Babylon and Sumer, the modern-day country of Iraq, to be challenging and perhaps even dangerous. However, those who do make the journey will most definitely still find the rugged desert land from the ancient dragon stories as well as the lush, fertile areas along the Tigris and Euphrates rivers. This land echoes with the ancients and still remembers the time of the oldest dragons. While many ruins have been destroyed by vandalism, flooding, and the harsh elements of this land, there are still ways and means to experience the energy of these ancient dragons.

The ruins of the ancient city of Babylon, chief city of worship for the god Marduk, are located about sixty miles southwest of Baghdad. The ancient walls and building ruins are well worn by erosion, although there have been recent efforts made to better protect them. The site is massive and is an interesting mix of actual ruin and replica. Ancient cuneiform, barely visible but

---

4. Richard H. Wilkinson, *The Complete Gods and Goddesses of Ancient Egypt* (London: Thames & Hudson, 2017), 222; Raymond O. Faulkner, "The Papyrus Bremner-Rhind Papyrus: III: D. The Book of Overthrowing 'Apep," *The Journal of Egyptian Archaeology* 23, no. 2 (December 1937): 166–185, https://www.jstor.org/stable/3854422; E. A. Wallis Budge, *The Gods of the Egyptians: Or Studies in Egyptian Mythology,* vol 1, *Studies in Egyptian Mythology in Two Volumes* (New York: Dover Publications: 1969), 325.

recognizable, can still be found on blocks of stone. Very few statues of any sort remain, but the sacred site is quite impressive. The earth certainly still holds the vibrations of thousands of years of memories. The path through the city that led to the ziggurat temple of Marduk is nearly perfectly replicated and can be walked by the seeker just as did the ancient priests in their yearly procession of worship.

The Gate of Ishtar, famous for its depiction of the dragon of Marduk, has been replicated at the site. A beautiful blue stone, believed to be lapis lazuli, a stone that was (and is) rare to this part of the world, covered the gate entirely, and the gate was massive: probably close to 50 feet high and 100 feet wide. The replica in Iraq is most certainly awesome to see, and the powerful energy of this ancient and mighty dragon is still quite potent.

As mentioned, the site is (currently) well maintained and easy to reach from Baghdad. There is a nearby tourist resort and car park. Along with a theater, museum, Saddam Hussein's (former) Babylonian palace, and the Tower of Babel (yes, *the* Tower of Babel), this area is rich with the ancient world energy and relics from that time.

An alternate method to experience the energy of ancient Babylon and the dragon of Marduk via the Gate of Ishtar would be to visit the Pergamon Museum in Berlin, Germany. The gate in Berlin is also a reproduction, but this one uses actual stones from the original gate *and* includes the inscription plaque from Babylon. The original parts were brought to Berlin after an excavation by Robert Koldewey was completed in the 1930s. Even more astounding, the museum has also reproduced the Processional Way. Here, the seeker can experience the grandeur of crossing the threshold and traversing the sacred path of the gods.

Ancient Hattusa, Modern-Day Turkey

Hattusa, the ancient Hittite capital, was the focal point of the battleground between the Canaanite storm god Taru and the chaos dragon Illuyankas.[5] It was also in this city where every spring the battle between Taru and Illuyankas was reenacted. Today, this land is known as Turkey, and the ruins of

---

5. Doug Niles, *Dragons: The Myths, Legends, & Lore* (New York: Simon and Schuster, 2013), n. p.

Hattusa not only exist, but they are a well-preserved UNESCO World Heritage site. Some of the precious relics and artifacts from ancient Hattusa can be viewed in the very nearby Boğazköy Museum. However, it is the Museum of Anatolian Civilizations in Ankara where the dragon seeker will find a brilliant carving of the battle between Taru and Illuyankas.

The sacred site of the Great Temple of Hattusa can be found in the Lower City of the Hattusa ruins. These city ruins are old, originally built in the thirteenth century BCE, and their energy is heavy with the echoes of the ancient and mighty ones.[6] The vastness of the city, simply the enormity of it, is awe-inspiring. For those who seek a connection with the old gods, the remains of the Great Temple of Hattusa are easily found and can be walked without interruption. Here, thousands upon thousands worshipped the old gods, and the land certainly remembers.

Land of Old Canaan, Modern-Day Israel, Gaza Strip, West Bank, and Syria

In the ancient land known as Canaan, there is a sacred mountain of the gods, a site where the land meets the sea and sky, called Mount Casius or *Jebel Aqra*. The limestone mountain rests on the present-day border of Syria and Turkey, with the Turkish side of the mountain being called Mount Kel.

This site has been a place of worship for thousands of years and was sacred to the Hurrians, the Hittites, the Akkadians, Phoenicians, and more. The mountain was believed to be an earthly home of the old gods; indeed, this was and is a threshold where the world of humans is linked to the realm of the gods. It was seen by the ancient tribes as the abode of the storm gods. Teshub, Baal, and Zeus were all worshipped here by different cultures.

It is atop this mountain that many believe the great dragon battle between Baal and Yam-Nahar of the Seven Heads took place. Indeed, in modern times, the site still vibrates with the energy of war. The site is wrought with frequent and intense storms that envelope the mountain's peak with brilliant displays of cracked lightning and crashing thunder.[7]

---

6. "Hattusha: The Hittite Capital," World Heritage List, UNESCO World Heritage, accessed May 14, 2020, https://whc.unesco.org/en/list/377/.

7. Michael Jordan. *Dictionary of Gods and Goddesses* (New York: Facts on File, 1993), n. p.

Excavations at the mountain's peak have revealed an enormous mound of ash and debris, which measure an incredible 180 feet wide and 26 feet deep.

Like many sacred sites, after the worship of the old gods was forbidden, worship nonetheless continued. The Christians built a monastery on the eastern slope where they actually reused stones, still stamped with Zeus's name, from the Greco-Roman sanctuary.

Tragically, the sacred mountain now sits in an area that is a Turkish military zone. At the time of this writing, it cannot be further studied, nor can the seeker safely commune there with the dragons. The intense energy of the battle between Baal and Yam-Nahar is still very alive and potent and clearly is being fed by the current war that humans are waging in that region. The land continues to be smote and torn as the battle between chaos and order rages.

Egypt

Egypt is a land of many mysteries and immense energetic power. The presence of the old gods is still strong and potent. The land seems to vibrate and hum from the energy of the ancient and mighty ones. For the dragon seeker who wishes to experience the energy of Mehen and Apep at a sacred site in Egypt, one can do so with little difficulty.

The protective power of the dragon guardian Mehen is perhaps best felt in a Temple of Ra. Fortunately for the traveler, the temples of Ra are numerous. The great temple of Karnak (actually a temple complex dedicated to several Egyptian gods) is probably the best known and is located in Luxor. This complex is, in a word, *massive*.

The Precinct of Amon-Ra is almost in the center of the complex. This is a very busy tourist spot, so having a private moment to meditate upon the gods and connect with the dragons is indeed a challenge. However, a private tour can be arranged with most tour agencies along with a request to have a few precious minutes of semiprivacy. In general, the temple complex is busiest in the cooler parts of the day.

Of course, with Ra being a solar deity, his energy can be felt in any location where the sun is shining. It can be a powerful experience to stand upon the sands of Egypt, the sun's rays reaching down to the earth, and imagine

Ra sailing across the sky in his sun boat with Mehen guarding him under his watchful gaze.

The energy of Apep, enemy of Ra, is a rather twofold experience. As Apep was and is seen as a direct challenger to Ra and the guardian dragon, Mehen, the seeker will not find any temples dedicated to this serpent. In fact, the temple energy that is linked to Apep has the echoes of the struggle between Apep and Ra and the annual ritual that the priests of Ra performed to hold Apep's power at bay. It is not the "pure" energy of Apep as a chaos dragon that one experiences; it is the *tension* between chaos and order.

COMMUNING WITH THE ANCESTOR DRAGONS ON SAMHAIN

Lore shows that the oldest of dragons, those ancient and mighty dragons, were there at the great beginning and even helped create the world. Their lessons of wisdom, silence, and transformation have been read and acknowledged. Using sacred space, you can approach and honor the ancestor dragons.

At Samhain, many magickal practitioners prepare altars and rituals for the ancestors for the purpose of honoring them. The following rituals, either the simple or more complex one, achieve something similar. We will first honor the spirit of the ancestor dragon in ritual. The ancestor dragon embodies the memories, the history, the long path behind us that has been forged by those who have come before us. We will then actively seek the spirit of the ancestor dragon in meditation and establish a communion that will open the gateways to a great wealth of wisdom.

ANCESTOR DRAGON RITUAL OIL AND INCENSE

Before either ritual, you will need to prepare the necessary oil and incense. First, prepare the ancestor dragon oil. You will need:

- 2 tablespoons consecrated frankincense oil
- 7 drops consecrated dragon's blood oil

- 5 drops consecrated patchouli oil

- 3 drops consecrated sandalwood oil

- 1 drop consecrated water

- 3 breaths (yours) upon the mixed oils

- 3 drops of lavender oil (lavender represents the spirit of the ancestors)

Take the oils and water and combine to make the ancestor dragon oil. Once the oils and water are combined in a container, hold the container in your left hand. Outstretch your right hand and hold over the bowl; speak these words:

I declare this oil as sacred to my purpose.

Pause for three breaths. Then speak the chant:

Hail to the ancestors.
We honor your sacrifice.
We honor your wisdom.

Next, prepare the ancestor dragon incense. You will need:

- 2 tablespoons of dragon's blood resin

- ⅓ teaspoon of patchouli

- ⅓ teaspoon of frankincense

- ⅓ teaspoon of lavender

Take the ingredients and combine in a container to make the ancestor dragon incense. Once combined, hold the container in your left hand. Outstretch your right hand and hold over the bowl; speak these words:

I declare this incense as sacred to my purpose.

SIMPLE ANCESTOR DRAGON COMMUNION RITUAL

The recommended time to do this is late evening. It takes about one hour. Along with the ancestor dragon oil and incense, you will need:

- Dragon candles (3): Purple for spirit, white and black for the ancestor dragons
- Incense burning container: A heat-proof container with 2–3 charcoal disks
- Offering of gratitude to the ancestor dragons: A small bag containing ancestor dragon incense. Place the offering in tissue paper and tie it to close.

Light the charcoal. When the coals are red, place a pinch of the incense onto the burning charcoal.

Light the purple spirit dragon candle and speak:

Here lies the place where the dragon dwells.
Here is an entrance to the Cavern of Crystal, Scale, and Stone.
Here gather the ancient and mighty dragons of old.

Light the white and black ancestor dragon candles and speak:

Hail to the ancient and mighty dragons.
Dragons of the sacred breath,
Dragons of the sacred flame,
Dragons of the sacred water,
Dragons of the sacred earth.
We come to you in peace.
We call to you in friendship.
We ask for your wisdom and guidance.
Ancient and mighty dragons,
We call to you!

Now, you are ready to experience the ancestor dragon meditation. When you have completed the meditation, write down your journal entries. You may also want to:

- Take the time to write a poem or song in honor of your ancestors or the ancient and mighty dragons. Record this in your journal.
- Speak the names of your honored ancestors. Honor them with a brief period of silence after their names have been spoken.

When your communion with the ancestor dragon is complete, place the gratitude offering onto the burning charcoal. Speak your thanks:

> *Hail to the ancient and mighty dragons*
> *Dragons of the sacred breath,*
> *Dragons of the sacred flame,*
> *Dragons of the sacred water,*
> *Dragons of the sacred earth.*
> *We have communed with you in peace*
> *We have joined to you in friendship*
> *We heed your wisdom and guidance*
> *Ancient and mighty dragons*
> *We thank you for these mighty gifts.*

If possible, allow the three dragon candles to burn down. If not, extinguish them until they can be (safely) allowed to burn completely.

FULL ANCESTOR DRAGON COMMUNION RITUAL

Like the simple version, the recommended time to do this is late evening. It can be done with a group or as a solitary. It takes about one hour.

Along with the ancestor dragon oil and incense, you will need:

- Altar candles: Purple for spirit, white and black for the ancestor dragons
- Elemental dragon call: Chime or bell for quarter calls (if desired)
- Ritual fire: Prepared for lighting but not yet lit

- Seeker candles: A small white and black candle (for each participant)
- Incense burning container: A heat-proof container with 2–3 charcoal disks
- Offering of gratitude to the ancestor dragons: A small bag of the ancestor dragon incense (for each participant). It is recommended to place the offering in tissue paper and tie it to close.

Place all of the items upon the altar. Anoint all of the tools for the ritual, including the candles, with a touch of the ancestor dragon oil.

Light the charcoal. When the coals are red, place a pinch of the incense onto the burning charcoal.

Light the purple spirit dragon candle and speak:

Here lies the place where the dragon dwells.
Here is an entrance to the Cavern of Crystal, Scale, and Stone.
Here gather the ancient and mighty dragons of old.

Cast the circle and call the elemental dragons, as outlined in chapter one. Stand before the altar and light the black and white candles and speak:

Hail to the ancient and mighty dragons.
Dragons of the sacred breath,
Dragons of the sacred flame,
Dragons of the sacred water,
Dragons of the sacred earth.
We come to you in peace.
We call to you in friendship.
We ask for your wisdom and guidance.
Ancient and mighty dragons,
We call to you!

Bow before the altar.

If this is a group ritual, give each participant a small white and a black candle; otherwise, take a white candle and a black candle into each hand.

Facilitator speaks:

> *Welcome to our celebration of the ancestors! The ancestor*
> *dragon is the spirit of all the mighty ones who have crossed*
> *the veil. The ancestors possess the wisdom of all the ages*
> *of the world, above and below. Tonight, we honor*
> *them and pray for that wisdom to guide us.*

Light the white candles and speak:

> *Hail to the ancestors,*
> *We call you to join us this night.*
> *We honor your sacrifice,*
> *We honor your wisdom,*
> *Hail to you, the spirits of our ancestors*

If you have a ritual fire prepared, light the ritual fire and place the white candles in or around the ritual fire.

Light the black candles and speak:

> *Hail to the ancient and mighty dragons.*
> *Dragons of the sacred breath,*
> *Dragons of the sacred flame,*
> *Dragons of the sacred water,*
> *Dragons of the sacred earth.*

Place the black candles around or in the ritual fire.

At this point in the ritual, you can experience the ancestor dragon meditation shared near the end of this chapter, or share poetry, story, or song while still in the sacred space. Here are some other suggested workings:

• Gather around the fire and celebrate your own ancestors with stories and pictures. Allow your emotions to intertwine with good memories and feel that love again.

- Take the time to write a poem or song in honor of your ancestors or the ancient and mighty dragons. If in a group setting, share while gathered around the ritual fire.
- Simply speak the names of honored ancestors and ancient and mighty ones around the fire. Honor them all with a time of silence after their names have been spoken.

After the meditation, workings, and shared poems and tales are complete, give each participant one of the small bags of incense as a gratitude offering. Hold the bags in cupped hands while still gathered around the ritual fire or burning candles.

Facilitator speaks and the participants repeat:

> *Hail to the ancestor dragon!*
> *Fly high and spread your wings!*
> *Bless us with wisdom*
> *Let us know humility*
> *May our service to you be true.*
> *Hail to you, the ancestor dragon!*

Toss the gratitude offerings into the ritual fire, or burn them later if no ritual fire is being used.

Return to the altar and speak:

> *Hail to the ancient and mighty dragons.*
> *Dragons of the sacred breath,*
> *Dragons of the sacred flame,*
> *Dragons of the sacred water,*
> *Dragons of the sacred earth.*
> *We have communed with you in peace.*
> *We have joined to you in friendship.*
> *We heed your wisdom and guidance.*
> *Ancient and mighty dragons,*
> *We thank you for these mighty gifts.*

Facilitator walks clockwise around the circle. Bow at each quarter and silently thank the elemental dragons. When back at the altar, bow again.

If possible, allow the altar candles to burn down. If not, place them in the ritual fire or extinguish them until they can be (safely) allowed to burn completely.

MEETING AN ANCESTOR DRAGON
THROUGH MEDITATION

The following meditation can be performed in one of the rituals or outside of ritual. If you are experiencing this meditation alone, record the meditation or have someone you trust read it to you during this communion with the dragons.

Whether alone or with a group during ritual, perform this meditation in your sacred space. Ensure that your surroundings are quiet and that you are completely comfortable (temperature, clothing choice, sitting or lying down, etc.). Make sure that this experience will not be spoiled by mundane annoyances!

Close your eyes and breathe deeply. Allow the cares and concerns of the mundane world to roll away from your neck... your shoulders... your arms... your fingers. Allow your back to relax, from your neck down, down, down, to the base of your spine ... and just breathe ....

Allow your focus to rest behind your closed eyes as you feel your body relax completely. You are still. You are quiet.

In your mind's eye, see yourself on a rocky hillside. It is late in the night. The stars are brilliant overhead. The world is deep in slumber.

The scatterings of grass are covered in a light frost. The air is clear, fresh, and has a crisp edge. The sun is warm upon your face. The energy of this place, of this time, is solid, good, and strong.

You stand at the bottom slope of a tall, snow-crested mountain. As you look up, you see a path that leads up the mountain.

Begin walking upon the mountain path, slowly, slowly, slowly ascending. Each footstep is deliberate and sure. Your breathing is deep and satisfying.

Take a few more steps and you will see the runestone. Take the path leading from the stone. Within a few steps, you see the entrance to the Cavern of Crystal, Scales, and Stone.

Look to the right of the cavern's entrance. There you will find a torch, lantern, or candle. Take the light and step into the cavern.

As you enter the first chamber, you sense the presence of the guardian dragon. Stop, remove your shoes, bow, and send a greeting with your name and your purpose for coming to the cavern.

Greetings, Ancient One.
I, [your name], come in peace and love, a humble seeker.

A black mist forms into the shape of the ancestor dragon.

Come, the dragon whispers.

Follow the ancestor dragon through the northern cavern passage. The passage is cold and damp, and the floor is of polished black stone. The walls of this passage are covered with thousands of citrine crystals and black onyx. The ancestor dragon walks ahead of you in silence.

After a few moments, you stand at the opening of three passages. The ancestor dragon enters the middle passage. You follow.

You enter a small, low cavern that is completely devoid of light. Your own light source is extinguished.

The cavern is much warmer than the passage that led you here.

Lie down, you hear in the ancestor dragon's gravelly voice.

Lie down on your side. The rock floor is hard; yet, there is a warmth and vibration there that soothes you. You sense something surrounding your body that is soft and slightly damp. It envelopes you comfortably. You feel safe and secure.

In the making, the memories begin.
The song of the ancients is sung
Again and again.

You begin to hear the whispered song of many, many voices.

We were born from the Sea
The First Ones
Tiamat
Mushhushshu
Kur
Illuyankas
Yam – nahar
Mehen
Apep
Born from the sea
From chaos
Creation and order did come.

The voices fade and you are left again in the warm, soothing darkness.

Sit and open your eyes, speaks the ancestor dragon.

Do as the ancestor dragon requests. Above you, a crack of light in the stone ceiling appears silently.

In the waking, light comes
With air close behind.
A new life mingles with the old.

Take a deep breath. You feel the now familiar warm and damp air fill your lungs … and then you shiver as the cool, crisp air from the crack in the cave's ceiling enters your lungs. At first, the cooler air is unwelcome, but then it quickly becomes refreshing. You feel invigorated.

Spread your arms and legs wide, says the ancestor dragon.

As you do so, the cavern seems to completely open. The ceiling, walls, even the floor, fade away. You feel the rushing wind all around you.

In the living, hearts beat strong.
Scales shine,
Fires glow.

For a moment, you feel as if you are a dragon that is flying high amongst a billion stars. You soar in silence, mighty and keen. The stars shimmer on your scales. Your wings beat, creating a song upon the wind.

Then, the vision fades … and you are back in the cavern.

Sit again, says the ancestor dragon.

You sit and relax, still breathing deeply.

The sleeping signals the twilight,
And the twilight brings the void.
In the void, memories join the story,
And the making begins again

You receive a vision of thousands of dragon bones in a deep, deep cavern beneath you.

Such is the great cycle, says the ancestor dragon.

Take some time to speak more with the ancestor dragon. Remember the smells … the sound ….

The time has come to return to your own world and
your own time, the ancestor dragon tells you.

Take three deep breaths. Concentrate upon the back of your closed eyes. With your next breath, you feel a shift in the energy around you. You begin to feel a bit heavier as you become aware of your body.

You have returned to your safe and sacred space in this world. You feel refreshed by this communion with the dragons.

Now, one more deep breath … and open your eyes.

THE WHEEL TURNS

Now that you have met the spirit of the ancestor dragon, take some time to reflect upon that experience. Although it is not quite the chaos of Tiamat's world creation, the vision of the dragon birth in the meditation is a powerful one.

Between now and the next sabbat, commune with the spirit of the ancestor dragon as often as you can. Use the meditation or simple quiet time in sacred space. Always have your journal close by to document each visit to the cavern as well as any insights that may come to you.

JOURNAL ENTRIES

1. Describe the voices that you heard singing the whispered song during the meditation.
2. Describe the sensation of flying amongst the stars as a dragon.
3. Describe your vision of the ancestor dragon.

CHAPTER THREE

WINTER SOLSTICE AND THE ICE DRAGONS

The Winter Solstice, Yule, or Midwinter, is most often recognized as the shortest day of the year. Upon the Wheel of the Year, this is a very quiet time when the bitter cold keeps most creatures bundled inside of their homes. The earth is slumbering and dreaming. This time is often spent in contemplation while accompanied by the soothing warmth of a hearth fire. This place upon the wheel walk is all about inner reflection.

It may seem odd to honor the cold and ice, especially at a time when warmth is essential to life itself; but remember that the snow and ice come from the sacred element of water. For the Norse, ice was actually considered one of the sacred elements.

LORE OF THE ICE DRAGONS

The realm of the ice dragon is hard stone, tall mountains, and vast caverns. These dragons are old (though they are young in the eyes of the ancestor dragons), and their tales contain doorways to learning balance, the value of sacrifice, and the gift of rebirth.

So, rather than focus upon the discomfort of the cold, at this point on the wheel, the seeker will be guided to embrace the beauty of the snow and the unique feel of the ice. Through story, ritual, and meditation, the seeker will be introduced to the ice dragon. Remember to look deeply so that you clearly see and hopefully embrace the lessons of the hoard-keepers.

The Norse hoard-keeper dragons are often seen as dangerous and wily creatures whose sole purpose, or so it appears, is to accumulate a vast collection of gold, gems, and jewelry. These dragons are clearly not a manifestation of the ouroboros; these dragons are the familiar image of the beastly dragon sitting atop a pile of gleaming treasure.

Yet, as we journey with the dragons, we should look beyond the obvious. Dragons can mirror precisely what we expect to find; or, we can dare to look past what our physical eyes can see. Yes, the hoard-keeper dragon is a feared creature; yet, he is also a creature that holds great knowledge *and* a key to transformation.

Fafnir, Ice Dragon

The tale of Sigurd the hero and Fafnir the dragon appears to be the traditional, Western European dragon-slaying tale. Yet, it most certainly is not. Here is lore that has many secrets that are rather in plain sight; at least, for the dragon seeker who dares to look beyond the obvious.

Sigurd's reason for killing Fafnir (or so he thinks) is to simply rid the world of a dangerous beast and become wealthy as a result. That is not the full truth, though, as there is a long history with this hoard-keeper. This dragon was once human. He was one of three brothers who all loved gold and wealth perhaps a bit too much. Fafnir's human story is quite tragic, but for now, we will move forward in the tale with the knowledge that this man's desire for gold transformed him into a nasty and vile hoard-keeper dragon.

It is the dragon's human brother, Regin, who has coaxed Sigurd to attempt the slaying. Regin's intentions are by no means honorable. In some lore, he simply wants Sigurd dead, and a dragon should easily take care of that. In other lore, Regin either desires the dragon's treasure or wants to eat the dragon's heart, sometimes both.

Fafnir visits a river every morning at dawn, and it is there that Sigurd determines to set a trap. As Sigurd is digging a hole in which he will hide and kill Fafnir, the gods decide to intervene and lend aid to the mortal. It is the Allfather, Odin, the one-eyed wanderer, who appears to Sigurd. Odin is disguised as an old man and advises Sigurd to dig a second hole. This second hole will allow the dragon's venomous blood to flow away from Sigurd and thus save the ambitious warrior's life.

Sigurd obeys the old man and digs the second hole. Sigurd then crawls into the earth and waits in silence for the dragon. This imagery resonates strongly with the expectation of birth from the womb of the mother. On a very deep and primal level, the man has willingly reentered the womb and is waiting to be reborn. In many esoteric traditions, this is called *initiation into the great mysteries*.

Sigurd's attack is successful, and he does indeed strike a death blow directly into Fafnir's heart. As he dies, the dragon speaks to Sigurd and advises the warrior that the treasure is cursed; he would be wise not to plunder it. The dragon dies, and Sigurd cuts out Fafnir's heart.

Regin had very specifically asked for the dragon's heart to be removed and cooked. Apparently, Regin intended to eat the heart of the dragon. Sigurd, oblivious and uncaring as to why Regin would want to do such a thing, does as Regin asked. He prepares a fire and begins to cook Fafnir's heart.

What happens next is quite miraculous and echoes similar initiation tales like that of the Welsh lore of Cerridwen and Gwion Bach: Sigurd inspects the cooking heart to see if it is "done" and burns his thumb while doing so. Instinctively, Sigurd puts his injured thumb into his mouth. In an instant, Sigurd is gifted with the language of birds. The nearby birds have an ominous message for the warrior: they tell him that Regin plans to kill him. Armed with this knowledge, Sigurd slays Regin instead and claims Fafnir's treasure as his own.

In later versions of the tale, Sigurd also takes the dragon's blood and paints his body with it.[8] The dragon's blood has the power to create an impenetrable magic armor for the warrior, thus making him invincible to any blade. However, like the dragon who has the one missing scale or the creature who has a single weakness, Sigurd's magic armor has one vulnerable spot: a single leaf has fallen upon his back during the ceremony, thus preventing the dragon's blood from mingling with his own flesh in that one place.

The knowledge of and from the dragon's remains thus saves Sigurd's life and makes him almost immortal.

It is quite clear that the heart of the dragon contains vast knowledge. By ingesting a tiny portion of the heart, the seeker has received a great gift: the dragon's knowledge has transferred to the seeker.

This seems to be a simple tale of a warrior slaying a dragon and ridding the world of a danger while becoming fabulously wealthy and famous. Yet, there is much, much more taking place. Sigurd and Fafnir are both transformed; and, in esoteric study, that is in no way a small thing. They have both been initiated and entered into a new phase of the cycle—their own life cycle and that of the world cycle.

Eating the Dragon's Heart

The image of Sigurd sucking upon his burnt thumb, or "eating the dragon's heart," is at the epicenter of Sigurd's transformation. The thumb is quite unique in that it is capable of both oppositional and appositional movement. In many belief systems, the thumb symbolizes willpower. For the young, the sucking of a thumb brings comfort and peace. It is a satisfying action that is akin to physical feeding and thus, fulfillment.

We see this image portrayed on many Viking runestones in Scandinavia and most frequently on what are called the Sigurd Stones. The image of the thumb in the seeker's mouth contains the echoes of other powerful tales of esoteric initiation.

---

8. *The Saga of the Volsungs.* Digireads, 2005, n. p.

As mentioned before, in the Welsh story of Gwion Bach and Cerridwen, the boy, Gwion Bach, burns his finger and immediately thrusts it into his mouth in an act of pure instinct. Sigurd is no different; it is not a *conscious* thought for him to "eat the dragon's heart."

Both Gwion Bach and Sigurd are "testing" a powerful and magical concoction to see if it is "complete." Both seekers have prepared the transformative ingredients, and *they both believe that the mixture is for someone else*. Gwion Bach acts as an apprentice of sorts and servant of the mighty goddess Cerridwen, so it is no surprise that his transformation is directly linked to his next interactions with the goddess. Indeed, it is this act that is the catalyst for the transformative experience. Like all change, especially metaphysical, it is uncomfortable. The pain from the burning of the thumb causes the seeker to act from pure instinct and ingest the magic.

For Sigurd, it is pure dragon energy. It seems that Sigurd does not have an obvious initiator. Unless, perhaps, it is Fafnir himself. Fafnir is the first non-human to speak to Sigurd, and though it is not embellished upon in the story, one would think that hearing a dragon's voice and understanding dragon language would be a miraculous experience indeed. It is certainly Fafnir's death and preparation of the dragon's remains that cause Sigurd *to* transform. It would appear, then, that "eating the dragon's heart" is a metaphor for initiation.

SACRED SITES OF THE ICE DRAGONS

The Sigurd Stones

Viking runestones are standing stones with runes and drawings that honor a hero or a god. Some runestones are undoubtably funerary memorials. Not all of these "story rocks" are standing upright; some boulders and bedrock also have the magic of the runes carved upon them. Some of the runestones have been relocated and many of those can now be found in Christian churches or museums.

Runestones are not limited to Scandinavia; others have been found elsewhere. It would seem that the Vikings felt compelled to leave their own unique "mark" using the magic of the runes as they journeyed throughout the lands.

To find a site in Scandinavia that is linked to the dragon energy of Sigurd and Fafnir is not difficult at all; the seeker need only to seek what are called the Sigurd Stones.

The Ramsund Carving, Sodermanland, Sweden

Sodermanland has been inhabited by humans since the Stone Age. Most of the religious sites here have evolved from very early forms of worship to formal worship of the old gods to Christianity and now, some Neopagan sites have been re-established. As you would expect, there are churches (modern and medieval), cemeteries, and runestones in plenty.

The Ramsund carving rests in a heavily wooded area south of the small town of Mora, Sweden. Mora rests on the shore of a very large body of water, Lake Malaren. To the east of the stone, a river outlet flows south. This may not be the actual site of Sigurd and Fafnir's encounter; but, the elemental alignment of this stone's location allows for the runic energy to be quite potent.

This is not a true runestone as the stone does not stand upright; yet, it does use the runes to connect with the tale of Sigurd and thus with the energy of transformation. The runes are carved within the coils of a Jormungandr who encircles the entire drawing. The symbol of the world dragon is significant; his presence on the stone indicates that this story is one of becoming whole.

The runes read, "Sigrior, Alrikr's mother, Ormr's daughter, made this bridge for the soul of Holmgeirr, father of Sigroor, her husbandmen." This seems to be a memorial intended to honor a loved one who has died. Interestingly, there is also the reference to the memorial being a "bridge" between worlds. The runes imply that the wife *transformed* the rock into an energetic conduit for her husband's spirit's passing. This runestone is something far beyond a mere marking stone.

Images from the tale of Sigurd and Fafnir can be found on numerous runestones; yet, this one is quite special: here, we have the culmination of the much deeper meaning of "eating the dragon's heart."

The dragon slaying tale is carved upon the stone and completely encircled by a much larger carving of Jormungandr. The drawing, left to right, begins with the depiction of Sigurd sitting by a fire and cooking Fafnir's heart. As he tastes the dragon's blood, the drawing shows the birds conversing with Sigurd and Sigurd cutting off Regin's head. Regin is next with smithing tools lying around his headless body. Next is a horse, presumably Sigurd's, that is laden with the treasure hoard of Fafnir.

The actual "slaying of the dragon" is quite an interesting portrayal: Rather than a rendition of Sigurd stabbing Fafnir included with the other carvings, Sigurd stands *outside* of the coils of the world serpent. His sword is actually penetrating and running through the body of Jormungandr. This can be interpreted as showing that the seeker is moving *through* the worlds in the journey to wholeness.

The carving "ends" with a dwarf that is very likely Regin and Fafnir's brother, Otr. The drawing can also be read in reverse; either way, at the center of the bridge is the tasting of Fafnir's blood by Sigurd.

The Gok Inscription

A short distance west of the small city of Gok, Sweden, not too terribly far from the Ramsund carving, you will find the Gok stone. Like the Ramsund carving, this stone is not far from Lake Malaren and is a large boulder that rests upon the ground.

Gok is one of the thirteen dioceses of the Church of Sweden and has a lovely Medieval cathedral sitting high atop a hill overlooking the city. This city was Christianized during the thirteenth century; so, not surprisingly, the Gok inscription has a Christian symbol that was probably added to the original carving.

The stone is a huge boulder that, unfortunately, has been broken. The carving is quite clear, though, and almost entirely still intact. Like the Ramsund stone, the tale of Sigurd and Fafnir dominates the carving. The entire drawing, with the exception of Sigurd actually stabbing the dragon, is encircled by what could be "two dragons." Whether it is two dragons or another rendering of Jormungandr is open to debate, but again we find the runes carved onto the dragon's body as it encircles the other figures.

Like the Ramsund carving, the image of Sigurd, sword in hand, is drawn outside of the dragon's coils with the sword actually slicing upward and through the Jormungandr figure. Just above and to the right of Sigurd is a Christian cross. Yet, the Gok inscription has been dated to coincide with the Ramsund carving; it was probably (at least originally) carved by an individual well before the Christianizing of Sweden.[9]

COMMUNING WITH THE ICE DRAGONS
ON THE WINTER SOLSTICE

At Midwinter, many gather around a hot, roaring fire with friends and family. We endure the longest night with singing, exchanging gifts, and the anticipation that now the days will grow longer and warmer.

Yet, this *is* the heart of winter. Outside, the sky is black and silent. The air is biting cold. Know that the spirit of the ice dragon dwells within this frigid landscape. This dragon *thrives* on the bitter cold. Its scales take the energy of the ice and transforms it into creativity.

We have read the lore of Fafnir and been made aware of the lesson of transformation. Now, using sacred space, the ice dragons will be approached and honored through ritual and meditation. As with the ancestor dragons, there is a simple and a more complex version of the ritual as well as a stand-alone meditation.

ICE DRAGON RITUAL OIL AND INCENSE

Before either ritual, you will need to prepare the necessary oil and incense. First, prepare the ice dragon oil. You will need:

- 2 tablespoons consecrated frankincense oil
- 7 drops of consecrated dragon's blood oil
- 5 drops of consecrated patchouli oil
- 3 drops of consecrated sandalwood oil

9. George Stephens, *Prof. S. Bugge's Studies on Northern Mythology Shortly Examined* (London: Williams and Norgate, 1883), 85.

- 1 drop of blessed water

- 3 breaths (yours) upon the oil

- 3 drops of consecrated peppermint oil (the peppermint is symbolic of the spirit of the ice dragons)

- 9 drops of consecrated ice water (if available, melted snow is best)

Take the oils and water and combine to make the ice dragon oil. Once the oils and water are combined in a container, hold the container in your left hand. Outstretch your right hand and hold over the bowl. Speak these words:

I declare this oil as sacred to my purpose.

Pause for three breaths. Then speak the chant:

Hail to the winter dragon,
Scales of ice and snow,
Bringer of the long night,
Lord of winter's cloak,
Hail to you, the dragon of ice.

Next, prepare the ice dragon incense. You will need:

- 2 tablespoons of dragon's blood resin

- ⅓ teaspoon of patchouli

- ⅓ teaspoon of copal

- ⅓ teaspoon of mint

Take the ingredients and combine in a container to make the ice dragon incense. Once combined, hold the container in your left hand. Outstretch your right hand and hold over the bowl; speak these words:

I declare this incense as sacred to my purpose.

SIMPLE ICE DRAGON COMMUNION RITUAL

The recommended time to do this is late evening. It takes about one hour. Along with the prepared ice dragon oil and incense, you will need:

- Dragon candles (3): Purple for spirit, silver and blue for the ice dragons
- Incense burning container: A heat-proof container with 2–3 charcoal disks
- Offering of gratitude to the ice dragons: A small bag of the ice dragon incense. It is recommended to place the offering in tissue paper and tie it to close.

Light the charcoal. When the coals are red, place a pinch of the incense onto the burning charcoal.

Light the purple spirit dragon candle and speak:

> *Here lies the place where the dragon dwells.*
> *Here is an entrance to the Cavern of Crystal, Scale, and Stone.*
> *Here gather the ancient and mighty dragons of old.*

Light the silver and blue ice dragon candles and speak:

> *Hail to the ancient and mighty dragons.*
> *Dragons of the sacred breath,*
> *Dragons of the sacred flame,*
> *Dragons of the sacred water,*
> *Dragons of the sacred earth.*
> *We come to you in peace.*
> *We call to you in friendship.*
> *We ask for your wisdom and guidance.*
> *Ancient and mighty dragons,*
> *We call to you!*

Now, you are ready to experience the ice dragon meditation. When you have completed the meditation, write down your journal entries. You may also want to:

• Take a stone with a flat surface and use paint, marker, or chalk to draw symbols, letters, or runes to convey a wish or goal.

When your communion with the ice dragon is complete, place the gratitude offering onto the burning charcoal. Speak your thanks:

Hail to the ancient and mighty dragons.
Dragons of the sacred breath,
Dragons of the sacred flame,
Dragons of the sacred water,
Dragons of the sacred earth.
We have communed with you in peace.
We have joined to you in friendship.
We heed your wisdom and guidance.
Ancient and mighty dragons,
We thank you for these mighty gifts.

If possible, allow the three dragon candles to burn down. If not, extinguish them until they can be (safely) allowed to burn completely.

FULL ICE DRAGON COMMUNION RITUAL

Like the simple version, the recommended time to do this is late evening. It can be done with a group or as a solitary. It takes about one hour.

Along with the ice dragon oil and incense, you will need:

• Altar candles (3): Purple for spirit, silver and blue for the ice dragons

• Elemental dragon call: Chime or bell for quarter calls (if desired)

• Ritual fire: Prepared for lighting but not yet lit

• Seeker candles: A small silver and blue candle (for each participant)

- Incense burning container: A heat-proof container with 2–3 charcoal disks
- Offering of gratitude to the ice dragons: A small bag of the ice dragon incense (for each participant). It is recommended to place the offering in tissue paper and tie it to close.

Place all of the items upon the altar. Anoint all of the tools for the ritual, including the candles, with a touch of the ice dragon oil.

Light the charcoal. When the coals are red, place a pinch of the incense onto the burning charcoal.

Light the purple spirit dragon candle (upon the altar) and speak:

Here lies the place where the dragon dwells.
Here is an entrance to the Cavern of Crystal, Scale, and Stone.
Here gather the ancient and mighty dragons of old.

Cast the circle and call the elemental dragons as outlined in chapter one.

Stand before the altar and light the silver and blue candles and speak:

Hail to the ancient and mighty dragons.
Dragons of the sacred breath,
Dragons of the sacred flame,
Dragons of the sacred water,
Dragons of the sacred earth.
We come to you in peace.
We call to you in friendship.
We ask for your wisdom and guidance.
Ancient and mighty dragons,
We call to you!

Bow before the altar.

If this is a group ritual, give each participant a small blue and a silver candle; otherwise, take a blue and a silver candle into each hand.

Facilitator speaks:

Welcome to our celebration of the winter dragon! Tonight,
we honor the ice dragon. Though it may be cold and bitter
outdoors, and the night is long and dark, the ice dragon is
strongest on this eve. The ice dragon heart beats strong
and hard; it is full and harbors great knowledge.

Light the silver candles and speak:

Hail to the winter dragon,
Scales of ice and snow,
Bringer of the long night,
Lord of winter's cloak,
Hail to you, the dragon of ice.

If you have a ritual fire prepared, light the ritual fire and place the silver candles around or in the ritual fire.

Light the blue candles and speak:

Hail to the ancient and mighty dragons.
Dragons of the sacred breath,
Dragons of the sacred flame,
Dragons of the sacred water,
Dragons of the sacred earth.

Place the blue candles around or in the ritual fire.

At this point in the ritual, you can experience the ice dragon meditation or share poetry, story, or song while in the sacred space.

Suggested workings:

- Individually, take a stone with a flat surface and use paint, marker, or chalk to draw symbols, letters, or runes to convey a wish or goal
- If in a group setting, have each person choose a word or symbol that represents the heart of winter and draw upon a large, flat stone with paint, marker, or chalk
- Prepare the fire offering incense bags with appropriate runes or symbols

After the meditation, workings, and shared poems and tales are complete, give each participant one of the small bags of incense as a gratitude offering. Hold the bags in cupped hands while still gathered around the ritual fire or burning candles.

Facilitator speaks and the participants repeat:

> *Hail to the ice dragons!*
> *Fly high and spread your wings!*
> *Bless us with balance.*
> *Let us know the value of sacrifice.*
> *Let us be granted the gift of rebirth.*
> *Hail to you, the ice dragons!*

Toss the gratitude offerings into the ritual fire or burn them later if no ritual fire is being used.

Return to the altar and speak:

> *Hail to the ancient and mighty dragons.*
> *Dragons of the sacred breath,*
> *Dragons of the sacred flame,*
> *Dragons of the sacred water,*
> *Dragons of the sacred earth.*
> *We have communed with you in peace*
> *We have joined to you in friendship*
> *We heed your wisdom and guidance*
> *Ancient and mighty dragons*
> *We thank you for these mighty gifts.*

Facilitator walks clockwise around the circle. Bow at each quarter and silently thank the elemental dragons. When back at the altar, bow again.

If possible, allow the altar candles to burn down. If not, place them in the ritual fire or extinguish them until they can be (safely) allowed to burn completely.

MEETING AN ICE DRAGON THROUGH MEDITATION

The following meditation can be performed in one of the rituals or outside of ritual. If you are experiencing this meditation alone, record the meditation or have someone you trust read it to you during this communion with the dragons.

Whether alone or with a group during ritual, perform this meditation in your sacred space. Ensure that your space is quiet and that you are completely comfortable (temperature, clothing choice, sitting or lying down, etc.). Make sure that this experience will not be spoiled by mundane annoyances!

Close your eyes and breathe deeply. Allow the cares and concerns of the mundane world to roll away from your neck … your shoulders … your arms … your fingers. Allow your back to relax, from your neck down, down, down, to the base of your spine … and just breathe ….

Allow your focus to rest behind your closed eyes as you feel your body relax completely. You are still. You are quiet.

In your mind's eye, see yourself on a rocky hillside. It is deep midnight; the world is completely silent.

The landscape is blanketed with fresh, powdery snow. It is cold but not unpleasant. The energy of this place, of this time, is solid, good, and strong.

You stand at the bottom slope of a tall, snow-crested mountain. As you look up, you see a path that leads up the mountain.

Begin walking upon the mountain path, slowly, slowly, slowly ascending. Each footstep is deliberate and sure. Your breathing is deep and satisfying.

Take a few more steps and you will see the runestone. Take the path leading from the stone. Within a few steps, you see the entrance to the Cavern of Crystal, Scales, and Stone.

Look to the right of the cavern's entrance. There you will find a torch, lantern, or candle. Take the light and step into the cavern.

As you enter the first chamber, you sense the presence of the guardian dragon. Stop, remove your shoes, bow, and send a greeting with your name and your purpose for coming to the cavern.

Greetings, Ancient One
I, [your name], come in peace and love, a humble seeker.

From the North, a silver and blue mist forms into the shape of the ice dragon.

Come, the dragon says quietly.

Follow the ice dragon through the northern cavern passage. The passage is cold, and the floor is of white polished stone. The walls are aglow with thousands of silver hematite stones and blue sapphires. The ice dragon walks ahead of you in silence.

After a few moments, you stand at the opening of three passages. The ice dragon enters the left passage. You follow.

You enter a vast cavern that is made of ice and snow. You can see the frost of your breath in the dim light, and a heavy chill is in the air.

Yet, you are not cold. In fact, you feel quite comfortable. The crisp air in your lungs feels invigorating; the ice beneath your feet is smooth and soft.

Come, speaks the ice dragon in a melodic whisper. *Look. See.*

Before you, in the very center of the cavern, you see the energy begin to swirl and move. Within a few moments, you see a small but warm campfire. Sitting next to it, stirring a pot of simmering liquid, is a young man dressed in leather armor. A sword lays near his feet. He looks very tired. His brow is creased with deep thoughts.

Come. See. Listen.

You walk to the campfire and kneel near it. Instinctively, your hands reach out towards the flames.

Welcome, stranger, says the young man.

As you stare into the flames, you begin to hear the whispers of other voices.

Here is the heart of the dragon.
Here is a path to knowing.
Sacrifice leads to gratitude.
Behold one who has the key.

The young hunter pours the contents of the pot into a silver bowl and hands it to you. Take the bowl. As the liquid cools, it begins to solidify. Amazingly, it twists and curves until it becomes the shape of an actual key, one that might open a door or chest.

You are not sure if you should eat it, take it, hand it back....

The wise seeker will ask, says the ice dragon.

You notice that the ice dragon is sitting across the fire from you, staring at you intently. In his chest, you notice a few scales missing.

What is this? you ask quietly.
Excellent, replies the ice dragon, *this is.*
What do I do with it? you ask.
Perfect, laughs the ice dragon, *you do.*
I do not understand, you say.
This is, says the ice dragon, *you will do and then you will understand.*
What will I do? you ask.
This, and the ice dragon nods to the key that is in the bowl.
Ingesting the dragon will lead to great knowledge, but you must
honor the sacrifice forever and always. If you take it with you,
you become a keeper of great knowledge and must always be its
guardian. If you gift it back to the dragon, then you will be
rewarded with a great friendship and trust.

Take some time to speak more with the ice dragon before you make your final decision. Then, do as you are compelled: ingest the key, keep it, or return it to the ice dragon.

The time has come to return to your own world and
your own time, the ice dragon tells you.

Take three deep breaths. Concentrate upon the back of your closed eyes. With your next breath, you feel a shift in the energy around you. You begin to feel a bit heavier as you become aware of your body.

You have returned to your safe and sacred space in this world. You feel refreshed by this communion with the dragons.

Now, one more deep breath … and open your eyes.

THE WHEEL TURNS

Now that you have met the spirit of the ice dragon, take the time between now and the next sabbat to deeply reflect upon that experience. The communion with the spirit of the ice dragon is a vision of birth, life, and rebirth through the dragon's eyes; however, you may find other messages via your own experiences.

You are also encouraged to commune with the spirit of the ice dragon as often as you can. Use the meditation or simple quiet time in sacred space. Always have your journal close by to document each visit to the cavern as well as any insights that may come to you.

JOURNAL ENTRIES

1. Describe the young hunter who was sitting by the fire. Did you get the impression that he had a name? If so, record the name.

2. What did you decide to do with the key?

3. Describe your vision of the ice dragon.

CHAPTER FOUR

IMBOLC AND THE HEARTH DRAGONS

Imbolc finds the seeker at the exact midpoint between the Winter Solstice and the Spring Equinox. In the Wheel of the Year, this is the first of the fire celebrations. Physically, the earth is still sleeping very deeply; yet, she is also just beginning to feel the urge to awaken. Preparation for that awakening, and ours, begins with literally and figuratively getting ourselves and our households "in order."

This position upon the spiritual path is the deep, deep dark of winter, a time when a single light can provide precisely what we need both physically and spiritually. This single light has the potential to grow into a warm fire or cook our food or simply allow us to see our world more clearly. The light also reminds us and fills us with the hope that soon spring will arrive.

During this time, most creatures, humans included, must shelter from the cold and dark. The focus moves from inner reflection to that of hearth and home, specifically, tending to the needs of our families and clan.

It is during this dark time of the year that the hearth dragon thrives. Coiled around the home fire as it burns steadily, the spirit of the hearth dragon is vibrant and warm. Its scales are perfectly numbered to bring balance to the home and allow the familial energy to flow with goodness.

This part of the wheel walk is intended to guide the seeker to invite the spirit of a hearth dragon into their home. Physical and spiritual preparation of the seeker's hearth and home will be clearly outlined. The lore and sacred sites of the Asian dragons will be explored; then, through meditation and ritual, the seeker will commune with the spirit of the hearth dragon. Through this communion, the seeker can invite a hearth dragon spirit to dwell within and protect their own home.

LORE OF THE HEARTH DRAGONS FROM THE EAST

The dragons from the Far East are powerful and benevolent creatures. They are very closely tied to the element of water and are said to dwell at the bottom of lakes, rivers, and oceans. Asian dragons bring good luck and are welcomed as powerful and noble creatures.

An important part of the Asian dragon lore is that the relationship between the dragons and humans must be kept in balance. Moreover, the dragon must always be honored. If the balance is intact and the dragon is respected, then good fortune will come.

However, the opposite can also happen. It is said that some of the worst storms in Asian history were the result of a human upsetting a dragon. The lesson of balance is clear: *the balance must be maintained.* This is a constant effort by the seeker in every aspect of their life. First, we will prepare the physical home for the welcome of the hearth dragon energy.

Be careful with how you place a dragon in your home; it is my experience that any visual depictions of a dragon should not have a dragon facing downwards or placed in such a position that the dragon cannot fly. To have such a representation in one's possession is an insult to the dragon. The scales of the balance are tilted and the world, micro and macrocosm, must react with an attempt to restore that balance.

This practice of living in accord with dragon energy is related to the Chinese metaphysical practice of Feng Shui. Feng Shui is an ancient practice that was (and is) most frequently used by the Chinese in orienting buildings, temples, and tombs, but Feng Shui is also used to build and arrange homes. The goal is to have a smooth and uninterrupted flow of energy within one's home.

If the seeker chooses to display representations of the dragon within one's home or in sacred space, be sure that the dragon is honored. With practice, the seeker will become aware of the energy balance and learn to recognize the vibration. Always seek to maintain the balance, and your home will be a safe and welcoming place for family, friends, and dragons.

SACRED SITES OF THE HEARTH DRAGONS

One only has to enter the country of China in order to experience dragon energy. Buildings, temples, fences, palaces, and personal homes are all constructed and maintained per the principles of Feng Shui and energy movement. Urban sites that are easy to visit include the Forbidden City, the Temple of Heaven, and the Summer Palace. These are very busy tourist stops, so finding a quiet moment to commune with the Asian dragons will be challenging in these locations.

To really get a taste of the dragon energy of this land, the seeker is encouraged to visit one of China's sacred mountains. The paths that lead to these sacred places are lined with temples, shops, and small villages. The pilgrimage from the base of these mountains to the peaks is not for the weak or faint of heart; these dragons challenge you in mind, body, and spirit.

Tai Shan, Guardian Dragon of the Sacred Mountain of the Dragon Emperors

The sacred mountain of Tai Shan is one of the oldest sacred sites known to modern humans.

For thousands of years, the emperors of China (who claimed to be the descendants of dragons) would make the pilgrimage to Tai Shan and then climb up the *seven thousand* steps (known as the Stairway to Heaven) to the mountain's peak. The emperor would be joined by both his own retinue and the common folk on this journey up the mountain. Today, the full pilgrimage up the mountain is made by millions of residents and visitors each year.

At the mountain's peak, the seeker will find the temple of the Jade Emperor and the temple of the Princess of the Azure Clouds. At the Princess Temple, people (mostly women) come to pray for children and to cure illnesses. The very old and very young all visit this sacred site; prayers and offerings are accepted and expected, and the seeker can linger in the temples without interruption. It is also believed that anyone who walks to the mountain's peak will live to be (at least) one hundred years old!

COMMUNING WITH THE HEARTH DRAGONS ON IMBOLC

For the observance and celebration of Imbolc, each communion, whether ritual or meditation, should begin in total darkness. During the ritual, the light will emerge in the form of candlelight and ritual fire. The light will provide clarity and warmth from the cold and the dark. From a symbolic view, the light provides hope and promise of what is to come.

We have read the lore of the hearth dragon and have been made aware of the lesson of balance. Now, using sacred space, the hearth dragons will be approached and honored. As with the ancestor and ice dragons, there is a simple and more complex version of the ritual as well as a stand-alone meditation. In these rituals, we shall honor the spirit of the hearth dragon and actively seek the spirit of the hearth dragon in meditation.

HEARTH DRAGON RITUAL OIL AND INCENSE

Before either ritual, you will need to prepare the necessary oil and incense. First, prepare the hearth dragon oil. You will need:

- 2 tablespoons consecrated frankincense oil
- 7 drops consecrated dragon's blood oil
- 5 drops consecrated patchouli oil
- 3 drops consecrated sandalwood oil
- 1 drop consecrated water
- 3 breaths (yours) upon the mixed oils
- 3 drops of juniper oil

Take the oils and water and combine to make the hearth dragon oil. Once the oils and water are combined in a container, hold the container in your left hand. Outstretch your right hand and hold over the bowl; speak these words:

I declare this oil as sacred to my purpose.

Pause for three breaths. Then speak the chant:

Hail to the hearth dragon,
We ask your blessings for our homes,
blessings for a fire warm and bright,
blessings for food hearty and good.
Hail to you, the dragon of hearth and home.

Next, prepare the hearth dragon incense. You will need:

- 2 tablespoons of dragon's blood resin
- ⅓ teaspoon of patchouli
- ⅓ teaspoon of sandalwood
- ⅓ teaspoon of juniper

Take the ingredients and combine in a container to make the hearth dragon incense. Once combined, hold the container in your left hand. Outstretch your right hand and hold over the bowl; speak these words:

I declare this incense as sacred to my purpose.

SIMPLE HEARTH DRAGON COMMUNION RITUAL

The recommended time to do this is late evening. It takes about one hour. Along with the hearth dragon oil and incense, you will need:

- Dragon candles (3): Purple for spirit, yellow and white for the hearth dragons
- Incense burning container: A heat-proof container with 2–3 charcoal disks
- Offering of gratitude to the hearth dragons: A small bag of the hearth dragon incense. It is recommended to place the offering in tissue paper and tie it to close.

Light the charcoal. When the coals are red, place a pinch of the incense onto the burning charcoal.

Light the purple spirit dragon candle and speak:

> *Here lies the place where the dragon dwells.*
> *Here is an entrance to the Cavern of Crystal, Scale, and Stone.*
> *Here gather the ancient and mighty dragons of old.*

Light the yellow and white hearth dragon candles and speak:

> *Hail to the ancient and mighty dragons.*
> *Dragons of the sacred breath,*
> *Dragons of the sacred flame,*
> *Dragons of the sacred water,*
> *Dragons of the sacred earth.*
> *We come to you in peace.*
> *We call to you in friendship.*
> *We ask for your wisdom and guidance.*
> *Ancient and mighty dragons,*
> *We call to you!*

Now, you are ready to experience the hearth dragon meditation. When you have completed the meditation, write down your journal entries. You may also want to:

- Bless and consecrate a dragon statuary that will be kept in your home (the hearth is an ideal location!) as an homage to the hearth dragons.
- Take a single log of wood and bless it with the hearth dragon energy from this ritual. Use this log in your home's fireplace (if you have one) to make a fire and bless your home with the protection and warmth of these dragons.

When your communion with the hearth dragon is complete, place the gratitude offering onto the burning charcoal. Speak your thanks:

> *Hail to the ancient and mighty dragons*
> *Dragons of the sacred breath,*
> *Dragons of the sacred flame,*
> *Dragons of the sacred water,*
> *Dragons of the sacred earth.*
> *We have communed with you in peace*
> *We have joined to you in friendship*
> *We heed your wisdom and guidance*
> *Ancient and mighty dragons*
> *We thank you for these mighty gifts.*

If possible, allow the three dragon candles to burn down. If not, extinguish them until they can be (safely) allowed to burn completely.

FULL HEARTH DRAGON COMMUNION RITUAL

Like the simple version, the recommended time to do this is late evening. It can be done with a group or as a solitary. It takes about one hour.

Along with the hearth dragon oil and incense, you will need:

- Altar candles: Purple for spirit, yellow and white for the hearth dragons
- Elemental dragon call: Chime or bell for quarter calls (if desired)
- Ritual fire: Prepared for lighting but not yet lit
- Seeker candles: A small yellow and white candle (for each participant)
- Offering of gratitude to the hearth dragons: A small bag of the hearth dragon incense (for each participant). It is recommended to place the offering in tissue paper and tie it to close.

Place all of the items upon the altar. Anoint all of the tools for the ritual, including the candles, with a touch of the hearth dragon oil.

Light the charcoal. When the coals are red, place a pinch of the incense onto the burning charcoal.

Light the purple spirit dragon candle and speak:

Here lies the place where the dragon dwells.
Here is an entrance to the Cavern of Crystal, Scale, and Stone.
Here gather the ancient and mighty dragons of old.

Cast the circle and call the elemental dragons, as outlined in chapter one. Stand before the altar and light the yellow and white candles and speak:

Hail to the ancient and mighty dragons.
Dragons of the sacred breath,
Dragons of the sacred flame,
Dragons of the sacred water,
Dragons of the sacred earth.
We come to you in peace.
We call to you in friendship.
We ask for your wisdom and guidance.
Ancient and mighty dragons,
We call to you!

Bow before the altar.

If this is a group ritual, give each participant a small yellow candle and a white candle; otherwise, take a yellow candle and a white candle into each hand.

Facilitator speaks:

> *Welcome to our celebration of the hearth dragon! Tonight,*
> *we honor the spirit and energy of the hearth dragon! As we*
> *endure the last of the cold season inside of our homes, waiting for*
> *winter to conclude and the first signs of spring to emerge, we will*
> *concentrate upon the energies within our own homes. We will*
> *remove any barriers to the flow of the dragon energy. We will clean*
> *and polish so that our homes are able to resonate with the light*
> *from the dragon energy. We will light candles to dispel the*
> *darkness. We will delight in the warmth and comfort*
> *of the free-flowing and healing dragon energy.*

Light the white candles and speak:

> *Hail to the hearth dragon,*
> *We ask your blessings for our homes,*
> *blessings for a fire warm and bright*
> *Blessings for food hearty and good.*
> *Hail to you, the dragon of hearth and home.*

If you have a ritual fire prepared, light the ritual fire and place the white candles around or in the ritual fire.

Light the yellow candles and speak:

> *Hail to the ancient and mighty dragons.*
> *Dragons of the sacred breath,*
> *Dragons of the sacred flame,*
> *Dragons of the sacred water,*
> *Dragons of the sacred earth.*

Place the yellow candles around or in the ritual fire.

At this point in the ritual, you can experience the hearth dragon meditation or share poetry, story, or song while in the sacred space.

Suggested workings:

- Bless and consecrate a dragon statuary that will be kept in your home (the hearth is an ideal location!) as an homage to the hearth dragons.
- Take a single log of wood and bless it with the hearth dragon energy from this ritual. Use this log in your home's fireplace (if you have one) to make a fire and bless your home with the protection and warmth of these dragons. If you do not have a home fireplace, use the wood in a future ritual fire.

After the meditation, workings, and shared poems and tales are complete, give each participant one of the small bags of incense as a gratitude offering. Hold the bags in cupped hands while still gathered around the ritual fire or burning candles.

Facilitator speaks and the participants repeat:

> *Hail and welcome to the hearth dragon!*
> *Fly high and spread your wings!*
> *Bless us with balance.*
> *Bless us with a guiding light.*
> *Bless our homes with your spirit.*
> *Hail to you, the hearth dragon!*

Toss the gratitude offerings into the ritual fire, or burn them later if no ritual fire is being used.

Return to the altar and speak:

> *Hail to the ancient and mighty dragons.*
> *Dragons of the sacred breath,*
> *Dragons of the sacred flame,*
> *Dragons of the sacred water,*

Dragons of the sacred earth.
We have communed with you in peace.
We have joined to you in friendship.
We heed your wisdom and guidance.
Ancient and mighty dragons,
We thank you for these mighty gifts.

Facilitator walks clockwise around the circle. Bow at each quarter and silently thank the elemental dragons. When back at the altar, bow again.

If possible, allow the altar candles to burn down. If not, place them in the ritual fire or extinguish them until they can be (safely) allowed to burn completely.

MEETING A HEARTH DRAGON THROUGH MEDITATION

The following meditation can be performed in one of the rituals or outside of ritual. If you are experiencing this meditation alone, record the meditation or have someone you trust read it to you during this communion with the dragons.

Whether alone or with a group during ritual, perform this meditation in your sacred space. Ensure that your surroundings are quiet and that you are completely comfortable (temperature, clothing choice, sitting or lying down, etc.). Make sure that this experience will not be spoiled by mundane annoyances!

Close your eyes and breathe deeply. Allow the cares and concerns of the mundane world to roll away from your neck… your shoulders… your arms… your fingers. Allow your back to relax, from your neck down, down, down, to the base of your spine… and just breathe….

Allow your focus to rest behind your closed eyes as you feel your body relax completely. You are still. You are quiet.

In your mind's eye, see yourself on a rocky hillside. In the east, the dark sky is tinged with indigo. It is pre-dawn. You can sense the anticipation for the coming sunrise.

The land is completely covered in ice and snow. It is quiet and peaceful. The energy of this place, of this time, is solid, good, and strong.

You stand at the bottom slope of a tall, snow-crested mountain. As you look up, you see a path that leads up the mountain.

Begin walking upon the mountain path, slowly, slowly, slowly ascending. Each footstep is deliberate and sure. Your breathing is deep and satisfying.

Take a few more steps and you will see the runestone. Take the path leading from the stone. Within a few steps, you see the entrance to the Cavern of Crystal, Scales, and Stone.

Look to the right of the cavern's entrance. There you will find a torch, lantern, or candle. Take the light and step into the cavern.

As you enter the first chamber, you sense the presence of the guardian dragon. Stop, remove your shoes, bow, and send a greeting with your name and your purpose for coming to the cavern.

> *Greetings, Ancient One.*
> *I, [your name], come in peace and love, a humble seeker.*

A yellow mist forms into the shape of the hearth dragon.

> *Follow,* the dragon whispers.

Follow the hearth dragon through the northern cavern passage. The passage is covered in white stone that is warm to your bare feet. The walls are covered with thousands of clear, quartz crystals and citrine. The hearth dragon lumbers ahead of you, humming a low melody.

After a few moments, you stand at the opening of three passages. The hearth dragon enters the right passage. You follow.

You step into a black void. There is no sound. No smell. No light.

Then, you hear a low hum. It is the hearth dragon. The hum becomes deeper and deeper until you actually feel the floor begin to vibrate beneath you.

> *I am born of thunder*
> *I come forth in the rain*
> *The rivers are my blood*
> *Mountains are my bones*
> *The sea foam is my dream*
> *I ride the winds*

Ever free and wild
I sing the song of my brothers
I dance the rhythm of my sisters
My presence makes wide sky complete
The darkness pleases me
yet I will bring forth the light
A quickening is beginning
A time to reflect
A time to shine by starlight

Suddenly, above you, the night sky appears. There is no moon; instead, a billion twinkling stars bring a silvery, dim light to your surroundings.

You can see the hearth dragon lying down close by; she is staring up at the stars.

You are made of stardust, says the dragon.
Sit and stare through time with me. The stars tell us the
great story. It is all above us, drawn by the ancient dragons.

Above you, the stars begin to twinkle and shimmer with renewed energy. Then, you see some of the stars begin to glow more brightly than others. The shapes of men, women, animals … and more begin to form. They grow larger as their shapes become more distinct.

Look, there is Draco, my ancestor.

The dragon nods towards the Northern sky.

Always seen, never hiding
Head of the Serpent
Guardian of the Golden Apples
Ladon, he was called
Set in the sky by Minerva
Frozen as he flew

> *Child of Gaia, he is Typhon,*
> *Mighty Titan, beloved son*

Take some time to gaze at the stars. Remember the shapes … their movement….

If you wish, speak more with the hearth dragon.

> *The time has come to return to your own world*
> *and your own time,* the hearth dragon tells you.

Take three deep breaths. Concentrate upon the back of your closed eyes. With your next breath, you feel a shift in the energy around you. You begin to feel a bit heavier as you become aware of your body.

You have returned to your safe and sacred space in this world. You feel refreshed by this communion with the hearth dragon.

Now, one more deep breath … and open your eyes.

THE WHEEL TURNS

Now that you have met the spirit of the hearth dragon, take the time between now and the next sabbat to perfect the balance of your home and your life. The communion with the hearth dragon is a vision of how we and all dragon spirits are connected to the stars. Through this connection, we can bring balance and light to the world around us.

You are, of course, encouraged to commune with the spirit of the hearth dragon as often as you can. Use the meditation or simple quiet time in sacred space. Always have your journal close by to record any insights that may come to you.

JOURNAL ENTRIES

1. Describe your first impression of the starry night sky.

2. How did the constellation, Draco, look to you?

3. Did you see other constellations? Which ones?

4. Describe your vision of the hearth dragon.

CHAPTER FIVE

VERNAL EQUINOX AND THE WAKING DRAGONS

The vernal equinox finds the seeker at a point of perfect balance upon the Wheel of the Year. With the arrival of spring, all life upon earth begins to awaken from a long slumber. In my tradition, the vernal equinox is a fire festival celebration. Physically, the earth is awake and ripe for the growing season. Preparations for the later harvest will begin with the blessing of the seeds. The planting of these blessed seeds, both physical and spiritual, will be an important part of this communion with dragon energy.

The dragons, too, are waking and breathing in the sweet smells of the season. As promised, the days are longer; winter's sleep is shed and replaced with eyes that will soon be wide open.

For this portion of the wheel walk, the waking dragons will be honored. The communion is designed to connect the seeker to the vision and power of these particular dragons.

We will use their stories, first and foremost, to familiarize the seeker with the dragons. Then, the teachings of the dragon will be highlighted. Finally, using sacred space, the waking dragons will be approached and honored.

LORE OF THE WAKING DRAGONS

In eastern Europe, dragons and vision are very closely connected. The mysteries of the seen and unseen, the power of invisibility, and the wisdom of being fully awakened are all woven into this brand of dragon lore.

Bolla, the Invisible Dragon

From the dragon lore of Albania, we meet Bolla, the dragon who strives to *not* be seen. The Albanian lore is quite revealing; the seeker is presented with a very precise overview of how Albanian dragons evolve and mature.

The lore tells us that if a female snake is able to remain unseen by any human for the first twelve years of its life, she will become a Bolla. The Bolla grows wings and wiry, red hair; she is not only able but also eager and willing to participate in combat.[10]

However, the Bolla still attempts to remain invisible to humans. If successful, the Bolla will then evolve into an *ershaj*. An *ershaj* coils around its victim's neck, opens the chest, and devours the heart. If the *ershaj* continues to live unseen by humans, she will become the mighty *kulshedra*.[11]

In the *kulshedra* form, this dragon is almost invincible. A *kulshedra* is most often depicted as having seven to twelve heads and female breasts. She is covered in red hair, has a long tail, and is fire-breathing. Her urine and breast milk are venomous. She can shapeshift, taking the form of a human, lizard,

---

10. Manfred Lurker, *The Routledge Dictionary of Gods and Goddesses, Devils and Demons* (New York: Routledge, 2004), 35.

11. Lurker, *The Routledge Dictionary of Gods*, 106,

frog, or salamander, as she pleases. She is a storm dragon; when she is angry, the world suffers from either storms or drought at her behest. It is only a human sacrifice that will placate her.

She has one true enemy, and that is the Dragua, the male dragon. The Bolla, in *kulshedra* form, will battle the Dragua to the death. It has even been written that Draguas will sometimes come to the aid of humans who are being attacked by the *kulshedra*. The battles between the Dragua and Bolla appear as great lightning storms.

From this lore, the seeker is shown the value of being both seen and unseen by others. Most importantly, though, it is the eyes of the dragon that truly resonates with this position upon the wheel.

For the dragon seeker, the lesson of being unseen and unnoticed corresponds with our journey. We shall view this cycle of becoming as akin to our waking from the dark of winter. We have sheltered ourselves from the elements and spent a great deal of time in darkness and quiet.

Now, it is time to gather the stored energy from the long winter's slumber and emerge.

The Blue-Eyed Dragon

Long, long ago, in what is now modern-day Albania, a sudden burst of wind upon the ocean caused a giant snake to emerge from the sea (evidently not yet a fully matured dragon) and it dragged itself across the lands.[12] The serpent moved inland and followed the path of water: lakes, springs, and rivers. The beast continued its journey, devouring humans and other animals as it travelled. Villagers were horrified and afraid, but they had no recourse for slaying a gigantic serpent. Except for one brave, old man.

The old man evidently knew a thing or two about dragons and had an idea. He knew that the serpent would shelter in a cave, if it could find one, and it would have to sleep, even if only for short times. So, the old man took a donkey and loaded it with sacks of straw. He found a nearby cave that

---

12. "Albanian Legend: How Was the 'Blue Eye' Water Spring Created?" Invest in Albania, July 9, 2015, https://invest-in-albania.org/albanian-legend-how-was-the-blue-eye-water-spring-created/.

looked like it might just be pleasing to a dragon, and there he went with the straw-laden donkey.

As he had hoped, the serpent emerged from the cave after its slumber. As he had feared, it immediately sensed their presence. The old man quickly set fire to the straw and hid nearby. The serpent approached the donkey and without a moment's hesitation, devoured the poor creature whole. The donkey did get a little revenge in that the straw somehow miraculously continued to burn *inside* of the serpent.

The pain from the burning straw was unbearable, and the serpent cried out in terrible pain. The beast called for its mother, the sea, and its sisters, the rivers, to end the agony. Yet, the sea was too far distant to hear his cries and the rivers offered no relief from the fire that burned so deeply within.

Across the mountains the serpent went, dragging itself as it cried tears of pain. You can still see the ugly and jagged scar of its passing upon the mountain, Mali Gjere, near the top.

As the serpent passed the water spring now known as Blue Eye, one of its eyes fell from its head, still weeping from the agony. The water from the tears covered the ground and went deep into the earth. Today, Albanians believe that the serpent's massive blue eye still rests in the center of the spring and continues to weep.

As with other dragon lore that we have (and will) explore, we have a dragon closely tied to a spring of water, surrounded by mountains and caves. Unlike the Greek dragons that so often guarded sacred springs, Blue Eye is not a serpent of the gods that is trusted with such a guardianship. Instead, this serpent *becomes* the spring and joins with the earth to form a place where sky, earth, and water all meet. Here, you have the energy of a dragon that has retreated into the earth and buried its sadness and pain deep within the roots.

Saint George and the Dragon

There are several versions of the tale of Saint George and the dragon, and they all belong to the dragon slaying motif. In all of the tales, there is a dragon, probably a female or *kulshedra,* that dwells near a lake and is terrorizing a small village named Silene. The dragon can only be held at bay by offering living, breathing sacrifices. At first, the villagers offer sheep, and they are accepted and hungrily devoured by the dragon. Soon, though, the dragon wearies of the sheep, and she rejects the offerings. The people of Silene panic and decide to offer the ultimate sacrifice: a human. In many of the versions of the tale, this sacrifice is a young, beautiful virgin.

George, a Christian soldier, comes to Silene and learns of their dragon troubles. George decides that the sacrifices must end. Using his (sometimes named) spear or lance, George slays the dragon and frees the town from their horrible plight.

In one particular version, though, George does not slay the dragon. Instead, he uses his faith to curse the dragon. As a result of the curse, the dragon remains "closed-eyed" except on Saint George's Day. On that day, the dragon can peer into the world and will devour any human who dares approach.

SACRED SITES OF THE WAKING DRAGONS
Blue Eye Water Spring, Mali Gjere area

The Blue Eye water spring is a sacred dragon site that can be easily reached by the dragon seeker. There are eighteen springs all around the lake, but the Blue Eye spring has a direct link to the Albanian dragon lore.[13]

The spring has a deep blue "eye" at its center that is surrounded by lighter blue on all sides. The mountain Mali Gjere can be seen in the distance from Blue Eye.

The site is not permeated with sadness or pain as one would expect; in fact, it is quite the contrary. The site is absolutely gorgeous, and on most days, creatures of all kinds, including humans, can be found admiring and even swimming or diving in the cool and clear water. The Blue Eye is the largest spring of the lake. In fact, Blue Eye is a national monument of Albania.

Energetically, what seems to be happening in this location is a vibrant evolution. This spring was formed from the tears of a suffering beast, our Albanian dragon, whose presence was not exactly in rhythm or balance with anyone or anything. The imbalance brought chaos and pain to the earth and humans, and the balance simply had to be restored.

---

13. "Albanian Legend: How Was the "Blue Eye" Water Spring Created?"

Despite, or perhaps because of, the dragon *being* the chaos, a sacrifice directly *from* the dragon was necessary to equalize the tension. Thus, one of its translucent blue eyes was lost and became what is now a beautiful, peaceful place where the elements meet in gentleness and love.

Saint Nicholas Monastery Church, Mesopotam

Very near the modern-day Albanian village of Mesopotam rests a very interesting sacred site that resonates with dragon energy. Currently, this site is an abandoned Christian Orthodox monastery that is dedicated to Saint George.

The monastery structure was constructed in the early thirteenth century. Judging by the diverse architecture, experts believe that the monastery was used as a site of worship by both Orthodox *and* Catholic worshippers.[14] Perhaps their reasoning for such a unique and bold project is that this site was once the site of a much, much older (and undoubtedly Pagan) temple. Hellenic stones have been identified from this ancient temple and are believed to date from the third or fourth century BCE.

The part of the monastery where most of these ancient stones were located is now called the Saint Nicholas Monastery Church. It is in this church where we find the clues for our dragons. Upon two separate walls are two very recognizable dragon figures. One carving has the dragon in what appears to be a resting position, mouth agape, and its tail coiled around its neck and along its spine. There are no visible wings, and one could well interpret the dragon to be in distress.

The second carving has a very similar dragon, but this one has very obvious wings. The dragon appears to be in motion with its forefeet stretched out before it. The mouth is wide open, and the tongue is protruding. The tail is coiled, but this time the coil is a single knot that is well behind the dragon's body.

It is very likely that the dragon connection of the church is connected to the full name of the entire monastery complex: The Monastery of Saint

---

14. "Monastery of St. Nicolas," St. Nicholas Center, accessed May 15, 2020, https://www.stnicholascenter.org/gazetteer/2929; "St. Nicholas (Mesopotam) Monastery," Into Albania, accessed May 15, 2020, https://www.intoalbania.com/attraction/st-nicholas-mesopotam-monastery/.

George. The dragon tale was known in the Georgian and Albanian regions as early as the eleventh century and eventually spread to Europe a hundred or so years later.

The sacred site of Saint Nicholas Monastery Church is abandoned and is not open to the public. However, visitors can contact the papas of the modern Orthodox church in Mesopotam to arrange a supervised visit.

COMMUNING WITH THE WAKING DRAGONS ON THE VERNAL EQUINOX

Winter is over! The spirit of the waking dragon greets us with fresh, white scales that are tinged with purple. The energy of the waking dragon, like the air, is crisp and clean. Winter's slumber has been deep and refreshing; we have empowered our homes, ourselves, and our families with rest and comfort.

Now, it is time to fully waken and venture forth! The world awaits your renewed vigor and strength. We have read the lore of the waking dragon and been made aware of the lessons of both seeing and being seen. Now, using sacred space, the waking dragons will be approached and honored. As with the previous dragons, you can commune with these dragons through the following simple or complex rituals as well as through a stand-alone meditation.

In both rituals, we shall honor the spirit of the waking dragon. The workings are intended to celebrate both the waking of the dragons from their winter sleep and prepare the seeker for the season of fire and creation. You can also actively seek the spirit of the waking dragon in meditation.

THE WAKING DRAGON RITUAL OIL AND INCENSE

Before either ritual, you will need to prepare the necessary oil and incense. First, prepare the waking dragon oil. You will need:

- 2 tablespoons consecrated frankincense oil
- 7 drops consecrated dragon's blood oil
- 5 drops consecrated patchouli oil

- 3 drops consecrated sandalwood oil
- 1 drop of consecrated water
- 3 breaths (yours) upon the oil
- 3 drops consecrated rose oil

Take the oils and water and combine to make the waking dragon oil. Once the oils and water are combined in a container, hold the container in your left hand. Outstretch your right hand and hold over the bowl; speak these words:

I declare this oil as sacred to my purpose.

Pause for three breaths. Then speak the chant:

Bless us with the spirit of waking.
Bless us with the flames of renewing.
Let us know the value of seeing.
Let us know the worth of being unseen.
Hail to you, the waking dragon!

Next, prepare the waking dragon incense. You will need:

- 2 tablespoons of dragon's blood resin
- ⅓ teaspoon of patchouli
- ⅓ teaspoon of frankincense
- ⅓ teaspoon of copal
- 1 teaspoon of dried rose petals

Take the ingredients and combine in a container to make the waking dragon incense. Once combined, hold the container in your left hand. Outstretch your right hand and hold over the bowl; speak these words:

I declare this incense as sacred to my purpose.

SIMPLE WAKING DRAGON COMMUNION RITUAL

The recommended time to do this is early morning. It takes about one hour. Along with the prepared waking dragon oil and incense, you will need:

- Dragon candles (3): Purple for spirit, two white candles for the waking dragons
- Incense burning container: A heat-proof container with 2–3 charcoal disks.
- Offering of gratitude to the waking dragons: A small bag of the waking dragon incense. It is recommended to place the offering in tissue paper and tie it to close.

Light the charcoal. When the coals are red, place a pinch of the incense onto the burning charcoal.

Light the purple spirit dragon candle and speak:

Here lies the place where the dragon dwells.
Here is an entrance to the Cavern of Crystal, Scale, and Stone.
Here gather the ancient and mighty dragons of old.

Light the two white waking dragon candles and speak:

Hail to the ancient and mighty dragons.
Dragons of the sacred breath,
Dragons of the sacred flame,
Dragons of the sacred water,
Dragons of the sacred earth.
We come to you in peace.
We call to you in friendship.
We ask for your wisdom and guidance.
Ancient and mighty dragons,
We call to you!

Now, you are ready to experience the waking dragon meditation. When you have completed the meditation, write down your journal entries. You may also want to:

- Take a blue stone,* place it in a bowl of water, and ask for the blessings of the waking dragon. Then, take the water and pour it upon the ground as an offering and bury the stone in the moist earth.
- Take blue stones* and ask for blessings of the waking dragon. Take a pen or marker and write the word "Awake" on the stones.
- * The blue stones need not be anything too expensive or flashy. Tourmaline, turquoise, blue agate, or aquamarine can be used to symbolize the waking dragon's eyes.

When your communion with the waking dragon is complete, place the gratitude offering onto the burning charcoal. Speak your thanks:

> *Hail to the ancient and mighty dragons.*
> *Dragons of the sacred breath,*
> *Dragons of the sacred flame,*
> *Dragons of the sacred water,*
> *Dragons of the sacred earth.*
> *We have communed with you in peace.*
> *We have joined to you in friendship.*
> *We heed your wisdom and guidance.*
> *Ancient and mighty dragons,*
> *We thank you for these mighty gifts.*

If possible, allow the three dragon candles to burn down. If not, extinguish them until they can be (safely) allowed to burn completely.

FULL WAKING DRAGON COMMUNION RITUAL

Like the simple version, the recommended time to do this is at sunrise. It can be done with a group or as a solitary. It takes about one hour.

Along with the waking dragon oil and incense, you will need:

- Altar candles: Purple for spirit, two white candles for the waking dragons
- Elemental dragon call: Chime or bell for quarter calls (if desired)
- Ritual fire: Light the ritual fire now
- Seeker candles: Two small white candles (for each participant)
- Incense burning container: A heat-proof container with 2–3 charcoal disks
- Offering of gratitude to the waking dragons: A small bag of the waking dragon incense (for each participant). It is recommended to place the offering in tissue paper and tie it to close.

Place all of the items upon the altar. Anoint all of the tools for the ritual, including the candles, with a touch of the waking dragon oil.

Light the charcoal. When the coals are red, place a pinch of the incense onto the burning charcoal.

Light the purple spirit dragon candle (upon the altar) and speak:

Here lies the place where the dragon dwells.
Here is an entrance to the Cavern of Crystal, Scales, and Stone.
Here gather the ancient and mighty dragons of old.

Cast the circle and call the elemental dragons, as outlined in chapter one. Stand before the altar and light the two white candles and speak:

Hail to the ancient and mighty dragons.
Dragons of the sacred breath,
Dragons of the sacred flame,
Dragons of the sacred water,
Dragons of the sacred earth.
We come to you in peace.
We call to you in friendship.
We ask for your wisdom and guidance.
Ancient and mighty dragons,
We call to you!

Bow before the altar.

If this is a group ritual, give each participant two white candles; otherwise, take a white candle into each hand.

Facilitator speaks:

> *Welcome to our celebration of the waking dragon! Today, as the sun rises, the world is in perfect balance. With this same sunrise comes a spiritual awakening; we feel an instinctual desire to open our inner eyes from winter's deep sleep. From dark night, we now see the stars overhead and watch them fade as the day begins anew. We are called to fully wake, feast, and prepare ourselves for the coming season. Today, we honor the waking dragon. The dragon spirit who aids us in becoming fully awake from the long sleep of winter.*

Light one white candle upon the altar and then light one small white candle for any other participants. Speak:

> *Bless us with the spirit of waking.*
> *Bless us with the flames of renewing.*
> *Let our vision be true,*
> *Let our awakening be full!*
> *Hail to you, the waking dragon!*

If you have a ritual fire prepared, place the small white candles around or in the ritual fire.

Light the second, unlit candle upon the altar and then light the second small white candle for any other participants. Speak:

> *Hail to the waking dragon!*
> *A great dragon comes with the power of seeing.*
> *Fly high and spread your wings!*

Place the white candles around or in the ritual fire.

At this point in the ritual, you can experience the waking dragon meditation or share poetry, story, or song while in the sacred space.

Suggested workings:

- Take a bowl of water and bless it with the energy of the waking dragon. If in a group setting, allow all to take some of the blessed water to work with during the coming year.
- Take a blue stone*, place it in a bowl of water, and ask for the blessings of the waking dragon. Then, take the water and pour it upon the ground as an offering and bury the stone in the moist earth.
- Take blue stones* and ask for blessings of the waking dragon. Take a pen or marker and write the word "Awake" on the stones.

  * The blue stones need not be anything too expensive or flashy. Tourmaline, turquoise, blue agate, or aquamarine can be used to symbolize the waking dragon's eyes.

After the meditation, workings, and shared poems and tales are complete, give each participant one of the small bags of incense as a gratitude offering. Hold the bags in cupped hands while still gathered around the ritual fire or burning candles.

Facilitator speaks and the participants repeat:

> *Hail to the waking dragon!*
> *Hail to the Waking One!*
> *Fly high and spread your wings!*
> *Let our vision be true,*
> *Let our awakening be full!*
> *Hail to you, the waking dragon!*

Toss the gratitude offerings into the ritual fire, or burn them later if no ritual fire is being used.

Return to the altar and speak:

Hail to the ancient and mighty dragons.
Dragons of the sacred breath,
Dragons of the sacred flame,
Dragons of the sacred water,
Dragons of the sacred earth.
We have communed with you in peace.
We have joined to you in friendship.
We heed your wisdom and guidance.
Ancient and mighty dragons,
We thank you for these mighty gifts.

Facilitator walks clockwise around the circle. Bow at each quarter and silently thank the elemental dragons. When back at the altar, bow again.

If possible, allow the altar candles to burn down. If not, place them in the ritual fire or extinguish them until they can be (safely) allowed to burn completely.

MEETING A WAKING DRAGON
THROUGH MEDITATION

The lore of the waking dragon has been explored and the lessons of seeing and being unseen have been acknowledged. The seeker is ready to meet the spirit of the waking dragon.

While in sacred space (or in ritual) clear your mind and let the mundane world's troubles and cares rest aside for this time.

If you are experiencing this meditation alone, record the meditation or have someone you trust read it to you during this communion with the dragons.

Whether alone or with a group during ritual, perform this meditation in your sacred space. Ensure that your surroundings are quiet and that you are completely comfortable (temperature, clothing choice, sitting or lying down, etc.). Make sure that this experience will not be spoiled by mundane annoyances!

Close your eyes and breathe deeply. Allow the cares and concerns of the mundane world to roll away from your neck... your shoulders... your arms... your fingers. Allow your back to relax, from your neck down, down, down, to the base of your spine ... and just breathe ....

Allow your focus to rest behind your closed eyes as you feel your body relax completely. You are still. You are quiet.

In your mind's eye, see yourself on a rocky hillside. In the east, the golden glow of the rising sun is magnificent. The warmth upon your face is soothing. The world is waking.

You can see new grass beginning to appear in the moist soil. There are flowers reaching for the sun. The air is clear and fresh. The sun is warm upon your face. The energy of this place, of this time, is solid, good, and strong.

You stand at the bottom slope of a tall, snow-crested mountain. As you look up, you see a path that leads up the mountain.

Begin walking upon the mountain path, slowly, slowly, slowly ascending. Each footstep is deliberate and sure. Your breathing is deep and satisfying.

Take a few more steps and you will see the runestone. Take the path leading from the stone. Within a few steps, you see the entrance to the Cavern of Crystal, Scales, and Stone.

Look to the right of the cavern's entrance. There you will find a torch, lantern, or candle. Take the light and step into the cavern.

As you enter the first chamber, you sense the presence of the guardian dragon. Stop, remove your shoes, bow, and send a greeting with your name and your purpose for coming to the cavern.

Greetings, Ancient One.
I, [your name], come in peace and love, a humble seeker.

A white mist forms into the shape of the waking dragon.

Follow, the dragon sings.

Follow the waking dragon through the eastern cavern passage. The passage is covered in smooth, clear quartz that is warm to your bare feet. The walls are covered with thousands of milky white opals. The waking dragon lopes ahead of you.

After a few moments, you stand at the opening of three passages. The waking dragon enters the left passage. You follow.

You enter a chamber that is warm and bright. The floor is covered in soft grass, and there are flowers of all colors and shapes blooming near the center atop a low mound. The waking dragon strolls directly to the center of the mound and sits.

Come, says the waking dragon.

Walk to the flowery mound and sit near the dragon. There is a light covering of dew upon the grass and flowers.

Let us sing to the new life.

The dragon hums and begins to rock slowly backwards and forwards. You then hear very distant voices singing sweetly from all around you.

We have set the sun to shine
We have set the moon to glow
We have the set the stars from far above
To light the land below

You find yourself moving in rhythm with the waking dragon, who still sits beside you. You are filled with a vibrant energy that is joyous. You can sense the growth around you. The grass and flowers respond to the singing with their own movement. They expand and grow taller.

You then sense the seeds that are below the soil; they, too, sense the energy from the singing and dancing dragons. They begin to vibrate and expand. The singing continues, and now the waking dragon's voice has joined the chorus. The voices grow louder.

We have set the sun to shine
We have set the moon to glow
We have set the stars from far above
To light the land below

The seeds push against the soil, pulsing with each beat of the song, as the grass and flowers grow taller. The scent of sweet, new blooms fills the air, intoxicating all life with desire and purpose. The song continues, and now, let your voice join the voices of the dragons.

> *We have set the sun to shine*
> *We have set the moon to glow*
> *We have set the stars from far above*
> *To light the land below*

The song continues, growing louder and louder, and the land responds with millions of new, fresh blooms. The seeds burst forth and begin to reach for the sky. There is new life *everywhere*. The energy continues to build until you sense the crescendo nearing... your skin tingles... all of your senses are fully awake... your rhythm is in perfect alignment with the dragons....

The anticipation is magnificent and envelopes the world with love and joy. As the land explodes with every color, the song stops suddenly, and the dragons and you enter a stillness. You feel the energy releasing into the ground and filling the currents of the earth's many lines of power.

> *It is done,* says the waking dragon.

In your mind's eye of your mind's eye, you see the energy travelling and covering all of the forests, fields, oceans, and mountains. The earth is absolutely aglow and fully awake.

Take some time to gaze at the energy lines and feel the power that they hold....

If you wish, speak more with the waking dragon.

> *The time has come to return to your own world and*
> *your own time,* the waking dragon finally tells you.

Take three deep breaths. Concentrate upon the back of your closed eyes. With your next breath, you feel a shift in the energy around you. You begin to feel a bit heavier as you become aware of your body.

You have returned to your safe and sacred space in this world. You feel refreshed by this communion with the dragons.

Now, one more deep breath … and open your eyes.

THE WHEEL TURNS

Now that your spirit is fully awake, take some time between now and the next sabbat to plant your own seeds, both physical and symbolic, for the coming growing season. The communion with the waking dragon is a vision of how our own spirit can join with the land and the dragon energy to help empower the land. Through this connection, the land will respond with gifts of bounty.

Commune with the spirit of the waking dragon as often as you can. Use the meditation or simple quiet time in sacred space. Remember to have your journal close by to record any insights that may come to you.

JOURNAL ENTRIES

1. Describe the song of the waking dragons. How did it make you feel?

2. Describe your vision of the earth with the lines of power, the ley lines, aglow with the energy of the song.

3. Describe your vision of the waking dragon.

CHAPTER SIX

BELTANE AND THE DRAGONS OF MAKING

Beltane is the exact point between the spring, or vernal, equinox and the Summer Solstice. This is a fire festival and a time for inspiration and creation. Beltane is an excellent point upon the Wheel of the Year to work with dragon energy to begin new ventures.

As always with dragons, balance is the key to a successful partnering with their dragon energy. For Beltane, the focus for this particular wheel walk is achieving balance between the seeker and land. In order to successfully implement that balance, the seeker must first understand the relationship between the dragons and the land.

Simply put, a successful partnership between dragons and the land is achieved and maintained by using the tension between the two. To understand this tension and how it works is perhaps best experienced by working and communing directly *with* the land.

LORE OF THE DRAGONS OF MAKING

The Asian cultures have observed and engaged in this partnership for thousands of years. The planting, growing, and harvesting of their crops, the gathering of water, the caring for their herds, all of this is performed in rhythm with the dance between the dragons, the elements, and the earth.

The Dragon Guardian of the River Min

Such is the lore of the dragon's pearl. Near the River Min in China, a woman and her son lived rather poorly. The son gathered fresh grass to sell to his fellow villagers, but this allowed the boy and his mother to just barely survive. When a great drought plagued the land, the boy had to travel farther and farther to find any grass.

One day, as he passed a dry riverbed, the boy espied a gorgeous patch of grass; in fact, it was the most lush and green that he had ever seen. He harvested the grass, sold it for more money than he had ever earned, and took the money home to his mother along with a fabulous supper.

The boy continued to harvest this miraculous grass until, on the sixth day, he decided that he would dig the grass up by its roots and plant it near his house. He dug all day and managed to get every sprig of grass and root. As he prepared to finish for the day, he found hidden within the roots and soil a beautiful pink and white pearl.

He took the pearl and grass home. He suggested that they sell the pearl, but his mother wanted to keep the beauty in their home for a while. She placed the pearl in a rice jar that evening for safekeeping.

The next morning, the boy found that his lovely transplanted grass had withered and was dying. He felt very guilty, for he blamed his own laziness, but then he remembered the pearl. He went into the house and discovered that the rice jar was overflowing with rice.

The pearl continued to bless them with good fortune. Eventually, their neighbors noticed that the boy and mother were prospering. The villagers were very happy for them; the boy and mother, in turn, happily shared their bounty with their neighbors.

Until one day, the boy and mother drew the attention of two men who were jealous and wanted the good fortune strictly for themselves. The men forced their way into the boy's house and demanded to know how and from where the good fortune had come. The mother replied that it was no secret; they possessed a magic pearl.

The men tried to take the pearl, but the boy swallowed it whole. Immediately, he began to suffer from excruciating pain and extreme thirst. He drank every bit of tea that they had; he drank the well dry. He ran to the river and drank every drop of water.

The sky responded with lightning, thunder, and wind. Rain began to pour from the sky. The drought was over. The people rejoiced!

The boy, though, began to transform. He grew horns upon his head as his body grew larger and larger. The mother and villagers watched in amazement as the boy became a dragon. He walked into the river and became the dragon guardian of the River Min.

The mother wept for the loss of her son; yet, she knew that his final gift (as a human) to the world was to fully transform and become something *larger than himself.* If he could no longer be a source of prosperity for his mother and fellow humans, then he had to allow himself to become something that could not only end the drought, but also prevent such calamity from happening again.

SACRED SITES OF THE DRAGONS OF MAKING

If a place exists where human, nature, and dragon all exist in perfect trust and perfect love, it just might be the Longsheng region in China. This fantastic area is a scene of *stunning* natural beauty.

There are sixteen hot springs where the water is so pure one can drink directly from the springs. The warm, soothing waters contain zinc, manganese, iron, and other elements that are powerful healing aids. While bathing in these springs at leisure, communing with the land, sea, and sky in peace and tranquility, it is easy to visualize a dragon slumbering beneath the rocks, its energy warming the earth and healing those in need.

Here the dragon seeker will also find Longji, which literally translates to "dragon's backbone." The dragon's backbone, when seen from a distance, looks exactly, and almost eerily, like the giant spine of an enormous dragon that is resting upon and between the slopes of the mountains. The dragon's backbone is where, six hundred and fifty years ago, the Chinese farmers dug hundreds of rice terraces into the mountain slopes. The terraces start at about four hundred yards above the valley and end in the clouds, just under a thousand yards above.

In the spring, when the rice is green and the winds blow, the dragon's spine dances and shivers with the energy of growth and life. When the rains come and fill the terraces with water, the spine becomes covered with dark and shiny scales that can be seen from a great distance. On those spring and summer evenings, the waters of the backbone beautifully reflect the night sky. Autumn finds the backbone covered in the golden "hair" of the ripe crops. It is winter that finally drapes the dragon's spine in crisp white.

The terraces are still maintained and can be hiked at all hours and entirely at one's leisure. Sunrise and sunset are especially powerful communion times at this site.

COMMUNING WITH THE DRAGONS
OF MAKING ON BELTANE

The spirt of the dragon of making is adorned with red scales that are tinged with orange and gold. The energy of the artist, the life-giver, the creator is strong with this dragon. "Making" is akin to birthing and changing; the dragon of making gifts the seeker with the energy for spiritual evolution.

As with the previous dragons, you can commune with the dragons of making through the following simple or complex rituals as well as through a stand-alone meditation. These rituals are intended to celebrate both the dragon of making and empower the seeker's goals and dreams.

DRAGONS OF MAKING RITUAL OIL AND INCENSE

Before either ritual, you will need to prepare the necessary oil and incense.
First, prepare the dragon of making oil. You will need:

- 2 tablespoons consecrated frankincense oil
- 7 drops consecrated dragon's blood oil
- 5 drops consecrated patchouli oil
- 3 drops consecrated sandalwood oil
- 1 drop consecrated water
- 3 breaths (yours) upon the mixed oils
- 3 drops of jasmine or honeysuckle oil

Take the oils and water and combine to make the dragon of making oil.
Once the oils and water are combined in a container, hold the container in
your left hand. Outstretch your right hand and hold over the bowl; speak
these words:

I declare this oil as sacred to my purpose.

Pause for three breaths. Then speak the chant:

Bless us with the fires of creation.
Bless us with the flames of the beginning.
Let us know the land dragon.
Let our lives become a part of the great balance.
Hail to you, dragon of making!

Next, prepare the dragon of making incense. You will need:

- 2 tablespoons of dragon's blood resin
- ⅓ teaspoon of patchouli

- ⅓ teaspoon of copal
- ⅓ teaspoon of dried jasmine or honeysuckle

Take the ingredients and combine in a container to make the dragon of making incense. Once combined, hold the container in your left hand. Outstretch your right hand and hold over the bowl; speak these words:

I declare this incense as sacred to my purpose.

SIMPLE DRAGONS OF MAKING COMMUNION RITUAL

The recommended time to do this is late evening. It takes about one hour. Along with the prepared dragon of making oil and incense, you will need:

- Dragon candles (3): Purple for spirit, red and orange candles for the dragons of making
- Incense burning container: A heat-proof container with 2–3 charcoal disks
- Offering of gratitude to the dragons of making: A small bag of the dragons of making incense. It is recommended to place the offering in tissue paper and tie it to close.

Light the charcoal. When the coals are red, place a pinch of the incense onto the burning charcoal.

Light the purple spirit dragon candle and speak:

Here lies the place where the dragon dwells.
Here is an entrance to the Cavern of Crystal, Scale, and Stone.
Here gather the ancient and mighty dragons of old.

Light the red and orange dragons of making candles and speak:

Hail to the ancient and mighty dragons.
Dragons of the sacred breath,
Dragons of the sacred flame,

Dragons of the sacred water,
Dragons of the sacred earth.
We come to you in peace.
We call to you in friendship.
We ask for your wisdom and guidance.
Ancient and mighty dragons.
We call to you!

Now, you are ready to experience the dragons of making meditation. When you have completed the meditation, write down your journal entries.

When your communion with the dragons of making is complete, place the gratitude offering onto the burning charcoal. Speak your thanks:

Hail to the ancient and mighty dragons.
Dragons of the sacred breath,
Dragons of the sacred flame,
Dragons of the sacred water,
Dragons of the sacred earth.
We have communed with you in peace.
We have joined to you in friendship.
We heed your wisdom and guidance.
Ancient and mighty dragons,
We thank you for these mighty gifts.

If possible, allow the three dragon candles to burn down. If not, extinguish them until they can be (safely) allowed to burn completely.

FULL DRAGONS OF MAKING COMMUNION RITUAL

Like the simple version, the recommended time to do this is late evening. It can be done with a group or as a solitary. It takes about one hour.

Along with the dragons of making oil and incense, you will need:

• Altar candles: Purple for spirit, red and orange for the dragons of making

• Elemental dragon call: Chime or bell for quarter calls (if desired)

- Ritual fire: Prepared for lighting but not yet lit
- Seeker candles: A small red candle and orange candle (for each participant)
- Incense burning container: A heat-proof container with 2–3 charcoal disks
- Offering of gratitude to the dragons of making: A small bag of the dragon of making incense (for each participant). It is recommended to place the offering in tissue paper and tie it to close.

Place all of the items upon the altar. Anoint all of the tools for the ritual, including the candles, with a touch of the dragons of making oil.

Light the charcoal. When the coals are red, place a pinch of the incense onto the burning charcoal.

Light the purple spirit dragon candle (upon the altar) and speak:

Here lies the place where the dragon dwells.
Here is an entrance to the Cavern of Crystal, Scales, and Stone.
Here gather the ancient and mighty dragons of old.

Cast the circle and call the elemental dragons, as outlined in chapter one. Stand before the altar and light the red and orange candles and speak:

Hail to the ancient and mighty dragons.
Dragons of the sacred breath,
Dragons of the sacred flame,
Dragons of the sacred water,
Dragons of the sacred earth.
We come to you in peace.
We call to you in friendship.
We ask for your wisdom and guidance.
Ancient and mighty dragons,
We call to you!

Bow before the altar.

If this is a group ritual, give each participant one of the small candles: red, orange, or red orange is recommended; otherwise, take one of the candles into each hand.

Facilitator speaks:

> *Welcome to our celebration of the dragon of making! Tonight,*
> *thousands of humans celebrate with hopes and dreams for*
> *creating children, growing crops, successful hunts, glorious*
> *victory, and more … it is a time of great hope and prayer.*
> *Tonight, we honor the dragon of making. The dragon who lends*
> *us the energy and knowledge to transform ourselves and our*
> *worlds; the dragon who aids us in riding the wings of creation.*

Light the red candles and speak:

> *Bless us with the fires of creation.*
> *Bless us with the flames of the beginning.*
> *Let us know the land dragon.*
> *Let our lives become a part of the great balance.*
> *Hail to you, dragon of making!*

If you have a ritual fire prepared, light the ritual fire and place the red candles around or in the ritual fire.

Light the orange candles and speak:

> *Hail to the dragon of making!*
> *A great dragon comes with the fires of the beginning.*
> *Fly high and spread your wings!*

Place the orange candles around or in the ritual fire.

At this point in the ritual, you can experience the dragon of making meditation or share poetry, story, or song while in the sacred space.

Suggested workings:

• A dance around the ritual fire is a fantastic Beltane ritual tradition! Either alone or with a group, stand (at a safe distance!) near the ritual fire. Focus on the flames. Turn and begin walking deosil around the fire. Either chant or sing as you move, slowly gathering momentum:

The days are growing warmer
Flames of beginning
Flames of creation
The dream is being fed

After five complete circles have been made around the fire, stop, face the fire, and allow the energy to settle into the flames. Take a deep breath and relax!

• Jumping the fire is another Beltane tradition that is both joyful and meaningful. Allow the flames of the ritual fire to die down a bit, or build a second, much smaller fire before jumping! If you or participants are unable to physically jump, simply pass near the fire with arms outstretched towards the flames.

• As always, poems, songs, and tales appropriate to the energy of the dragons of making are appropriate. Chant, sing, and play the bard in celebration!

After the meditation, workings, and shared poems and tales are complete, give each participant one of the small bags of incense as a gratitude offering. Hold the bags in cupped hands while still gathered around the ritual fire or burning candles.

Facilitator speaks and the participants repeat:

Hail to the dragon of making!
Hail to the One who blesses us with creation.
Fly high and spread your wings!
Bless us with the flames of the beginning.
Let us know the land dragon.

Let our lives become a part of the great balance.
Hail to you, the dragon of making!

Toss the gratitude offerings into the ritual fire, or burn them later if no ritual fire is being used.

Hail to the ancient and mighty dragons.
Dragons of the sacred breath,
Dragons of the sacred flame,
Dragons of the sacred water,
Dragons of the sacred earth.
We have communed with you in peace.
We have joined to you in friendship.
We heed your wisdom and guidance.
Ancient and mighty dragons,
We thank you for these mighty gifts.

Facilitator walks clockwise around the circle. Bow at each quarter and silently thank the elemental dragons. When back at the altar, bow again.

If possible, allow the altar candles to burn down. If not, place them in the ritual fire or extinguish them until they can be (safely) allowed to burn completely.

MEETING A DRAGON OF MAKING
THROUGH MEDITATION

The lesson from the dragons of making is that in order to feed the fires of inspiration with dragon energy, the seeker must first achieve balance with the land. It is time to explore this lesson through meditation. You can do this work inside or outside of ritual.

If you are experiencing this meditation alone, record the meditation or have someone you trust read it to you during this communion with the dragons.

Whether alone or with a group during ritual, perform this meditation in your sacred space. Ensure that your surroundings are quiet and that you are completely comfortable (temperature, clothing choice, sitting or lying down, etc.). Make sure that this experience will not be spoiled by mundane annoyances!

Close your eyes and breathe deeply. Allow the cares and concerns of the mundane world to roll away from your neck … your shoulders … your arms … your fingers. Allow your back to relax, from your neck down, down, down, to the base of your spine … and just breathe ….

Allow your focus to rest behind your closed eyes as you feel your body relax completely. You are still. You are quiet.

In your mind's eye, see yourself on a rocky hillside. It is midmorning; the sun is still climbing the sky wheel, and the world is just becoming fully awakened.

There is new growth all around you. You can see every shade of green in the grass and trees. Flowers of every color are blooming. Bees are covered in yellow pollen. The energy of this place, of this time, is solid, good, and strong.

You stand at the bottom slope of a tall, snow-crested mountain. As you look up, you see a path that leads up the mountain.

Begin walking upon the mountain path, slowly, slowly, slowly ascending. Each footstep is deliberate and sure. Your breathing is deep and satisfying.

Take a few more steps and you will see the runestone. Take the path leading from the stone. Within a few steps, you see the entrance to the Cavern of Crystal, Scales, and Stone.

Look to the right of the cavern's entrance. There you will find a torch, lantern, or candle. Take the light and step into the cavern.

As you enter the first chamber, you sense the presence of the guardian dragon. Stop, remove your shoes, bow, and send a greeting with your name and your purpose for coming to the cavern.

Greetings, Ancient One.
I, [your name], come in peace and love, a humble seeker.

A red and orange mist forms and twists into the shape of a dragon of making.

Come, says the dragon, *follow me.*

Follow the dragon of making through the southern cavern passage. The passage is very warm, and the sandy floor is smooth and even. The walls are aglow with thousands of citrine crystals, garnets, and rubies. The dragon of making's movement is lithe and smooth as it walks before you.

After a few moments, you stand at an opening with three passageways. The dragon of making enters the left passage. You follow quickly.

You emerge into a small, dimly lit cavern. In the center burns a single flame that hovers just above the sandy floor. The golden sand is soft and warm upon your bare feet.

The dragon of making walks and then sits before the burning flame.

Come, Seeker, and sit beside me, the dragon rumbles.

Go and sit beside the dragon of making. Take a moment to focus on your surroundings.

The single burning flame makes no sound.

This is the silence of creation, says the dragon.

The flame changes color and begins to hiss.

This is the beginning, says the dragon.

The dragon places a log of wood beneath the flame, which changes color again and begins to crackle as it burns the log.

The dream must be fed, says the dragon.

More logs are placed beneath the flame and soon, a hot and roaring fire is burning.

Here is the crucible of making, says the dragon.

The logs burn and morph into hot, burning dragon scales. Some of the logs twist and blacken and become dragon horns. Other logs glow orange, crumble, and become dragon eyes.

As you sit with the dragon, you receive a vision of hundreds, even thousands, of humans leaping over other fires of making.

> *The days will grow much warmer now,* the dragon of
> making speaks to you. *The seeds of hope that are sown
> tonight will grow. Tend your fire, Seeker; feed it. Guard it.*

Take some time to speak more with the dragon of making. Remember the smells … the sound … .

> *The time has come to return to your own world
> and your own time,* the dragon of making tells you.

Take three deep breaths. Concentrate upon the back of your closed eyes. With your next breath, you feel a shift in the energy around you. You begin to feel a bit heavier as you become aware of your body.

You have returned to your safe and sacred space in this world. You feel refreshed by this communion with the dragons.

Now, one more deep breath … and open your eyes.

THE WHEEL TURNS

The communion with the dragon of making is a vision of the cycle of creation. Starting with only a single flame, the seeker witnesses the dragon build a crucible of making.

By witnessing this vision, you have kindled your own fires of creation. You are ready to take this energy through the next six weeks until the Summer Solstice.

Commune with the spirit of the dragon of making as often as you can. Use the meditation or simple quiet time in sacred space. Remember to have your journal close by to record any insights that may come to you.

JOURNAL ENTRIES

1. Describe the flame of making that you saw. What color was it when you entered? What colors did it become?

2. Describe the logs of the fire as they burned.

3. Describe your vision of the dragon of making.

.

CHAPTER SEVEN

LITHA AND THE GOLDEN DRAGONS OF SUMMER

Litha, Summer Solstice, or Midsummer, brings the seeker to the longest day of the year. The earth is fully alive; the fields are full of promising harvests, and the life-giving warmth of the sun can be felt everywhere. Upon the Wheel of the Year, this is a vibrant time of activity. This energy is very warm and soothing; yet, it is also tinged with an edge of excitement. This time is often spent in vigorous activity and used for reconciling of conflicts. For this wheel walk, the seeker will focus on how they interact with the world and how the choices from those interactions affect the world.

Choices certainly always lead to results, or consequences as it may be. When a seeker is diligently walking a path dedicated to the gods, they often find themselves faced with rather challenging tests. The choices made during these tests act as conduits for change. For this wheel walk with the dragons, the lore and lesson focus upon not only the change within the seeker, but also for the dragon and for the world.

LORE OF THE GOLDEN DRAGONS

The image of a dragon lying atop a mound of gleaming jewels and coins is perhaps the archetypal image of the Western dragon. This dragon is empowered by his hoard and is dedicated to protecting it. These dragons often have a particular piece of treasure that he or she is particularly fond of or that they are tasked with guarding especially closely.

If the dragon acts as guardian long enough, the jewels and precious metals meld as part of the dragon's body; they can and do become encrusted into the dragon's flesh. Thus, the dragon becomes golden and jeweled in appearance.

Although they spend many, many years as diligent guardians, inevitably, someone appears who wishes to challenge them. More often than not, these encounters are initiated by humans in their various quests. When the seeker finally does encounter this dragon, oftentimes the gods will and do intervene with the tools to aid the seeker *and* the dragon.

The (Neversleeping) Drakon of Colchis (Kholkikos)

The Greek hero Jason, of *Jason and the Argonauts*, experiences a journey of transformation that involves a guardian dragon encounter. Although the tale ultimately ends in typical Greek tragedy, let us not forget that tragedy is a form of imitation that is more *philosophical* than historical.

Keeping that in mind, we shall look at Jason's encounter with the dragon of Colchis. This dragon is an old and sleepless guardian dragon. Deep within the sacred grove of Ares, the dragon of Colchis guards the Golden Fleece. The dragon is enormous; he could envelope an entire ship within its coils. He has one purpose: guard the golden skin of Zeus's ram, called the Golden Fleece.

Jason's quest is to obtain the closely guarded Golden Fleece. Jason has to, quite literally, face the dragon. We have three different versions of the encounter. There is a rather brute strength, heroic version where Jason simply slays the beast and wins the hand of the king's daughter.

In the more common version, the sorceress Medea, daughter of the king of Colchis, gifts Jason with a sleeping draught. Jason is able to put the dragon to sleep with the potion while Orpheus, a member of the *Argo*'s crew, plays a soft lullaby on the lyre.[15] The sleepless dragon of Colchis is thus lulled into a peaceful rest; a rest that he probably has not experienced in many, many years. The Golden Fleece is taken without incident, and the dragon lives to see another day.

Yet, it is the third version, known only by a vase painting from the fifth century BCE, that perhaps best symbolizes the transformation that is actually being portrayed in this (and other) dragon slaying tales: the vase clearly shows Jason being completely devoured whole *and* disgorged by the dragon of Colchis.

Jason had not *slain* a dragon, nor was he slain *by* the dragon; they both were *transformed* by the encounter.

Sowing the Dragon's Teeth

If Jason nor the dragon was slain, then what is happening in this tale? Where do we see the transformation of dragon and Jason taking place? A close examination of "sowing the dragon's teeth" is next in our lore lesson.

Sowing the dragon's teeth is a story motif where a human slays a dragon and then plants the slain dragon's teeth in the ground. This dragon lore is found in two Greek myths: *Cadmus and the Founding of Thebes* (see chapter nine) and in *Jason and the Argonauts*.

Just as with Cadmus' tale, Jason's "sowing the dragon's teeth" episode symbolizes the power of the dragon even after it has been "slain." The teeth give rise to a fierce band of warriors. Once that warrior energy is tamed, it can be focused and managed.

The dragon's teeth episode is not always included in the Argonaut tale.

---

15. Apollonius of Rhodes, *Jason and the Argonauts* (New York: Penguin Classics, 2014), n. p.

In some versions, upon his arrival in Colchis and declaration that he must have the Golden Fleece, Jason receives the dragon's teeth as a "gift" from the king of Colchis, Medea's father. Jason is told to sow the teeth and harvest whatever crop they yield.[16] If he is successful in his harvest, the Golden Fleece will be given to him.

Of course, the plough that Jason must use to prepare the field where the teeth will be sown is pulled by a troublesome pair of fire-breathing bulls. After overcoming that obstacle, Jason must then deal with the fierce warriors who grow from the dragon's teeth. With assistance from the gods and Medea, Jason successfully overcomes all of the challenges. The planting of a slain dragon's teeth is akin to planting the seeds of chaos. If the chaos is managed effectively, that chaos will be followed by creation.

SACRED SITES OF THE DRAGON OF COLCHIS

Unfortunately, the precise location of the Garden of Ares and the Golden Fleece is not known. However, by examining the geography of the region today and comparing it to descriptions from the lore, it is possible to locate several sites from the ancient world that may well contain energetic connections to the dragon of Colchis and Jason's encounter with him.

The Garden of Ares

We know that the Garden of Ares was within a grove of trees. There, the Golden Fleece rested within the branches of an enormous oak tree, and the dragon guarded it close by. As stated before, Kutaisi has trees in plenty and oaks are certainly among them.

It is doubtful that the Kutaisi Botanical Gardens are the actual site of the Garden of Ares; however, the elemental alignments would certainly allow the seeker to experience at least a taste of the energy of the dragon of Colchis.

---

16. Apollonius of Rhodes, *Jason and the Argonauts*, n. p.

COMMUNING WITH THE GOLDEN DRAGONS OF SUMMER ON LITHA

The summer dragon is adorned with golden scales that are tinged with red and orange. A shield of intense heat surrounds this brilliant creature; a heat that can provide warmth and life but also a heat that can scorch and burn. The golden dragon of summer is brilliant to behold and powerful to witness. As with the previous dragons, you can commune with the dragons of summer through the following simple or complex ritual as well as through a stand-alone meditation. These rituals are intended to celebrate both the dragons of summer and empower the seeker's journey in search of the golden dragons.

DRAGONS OF SUMMER RITUAL OIL AND INCENSE

Before either ritual, you will need to prepare the necessary oil and incense.

First, prepare the summer dragon oil. You will need:

- 2 tablespoons consecrated frankincense oil
- 7 drops consecrated dragon's blood oil
- 5 drops consecrated patchouli oil
- 3 drops consecrated sandalwood oil
- 1 drop consecrated water
- 3 breaths (yours) upon the mixed oils
- 9 drops of storm water (captured during a thunderstorm)

Take the oils and water and combine to make the summer dragon oil. Once the oils and water are combined in a container, hold the container in your left hand. Outstretch your right hand and hold over the bowl; speak these words:

I declare this oil as sacred to my purpose.

Pause for three breaths. Then speak the chant:

Hail to the ancestors,
We honor your sacrifice
We honor your wisdom

Next, prepare the summer dragon incense. You will need:

- 2 tablespoons of dragon's blood resin
- ⅓ teaspoon of patchouli
- ⅓ teaspoon of frankincense
- ⅓ teaspoon of sandalwood
- ⅓ teaspoon of red sandalwood

Take the ingredients and combine in a container to make the summer dragon incense. Once combined, hold the container in your left hand. Outstretch your right hand and hold over the bowl; speak these words:

I declare this incense as sacred to my purpose.

SIMPLE GOLDEN DRAGONS OF
SUMMER COMMUNION RITUAL

The recommended time to do this is late evening. It takes about one hour. Along with the prepared summer dragon oil and incense, you will need:

- Dragon candles (3): Purple for spirit, gold and white candles for the golden dragons of summer
- Incense burning container: A heat-proof container with 2–3 charcoal disks
- Offering of gratitude to the golden dragons of summer: A small bag of the golden dragons of summer incense. It is recommended to place the offering in tissue paper and tie it to close.

Light the charcoal. When the coals are red, place a pinch of the incense onto the burning charcoal.

Light the purple spirit dragon candle and speak:

Here lies the place where the dragon dwells.
Here is an entrance to the Cavern of Crystal, Scale, and Stone.
Here gather the ancient and mighty dragons of old.

Light the gold and white golden dragons of summer candles and speak:

Hail to the ancient and mighty dragons.
Dragons of the sacred breath,
Dragons of the sacred flame,
Dragons of the sacred water,
Dragons of the sacred earth.
We come to you in peace.
We call to you in friendship.
We ask for your wisdom and guidance.
Ancient and mighty dragons,
We call to you!

Now, you are ready to experience the golden dragon of summer meditation. When you have completed the meditation, write down your journal entries. You may also want to:

- If you have any jewelry that can be gifted (and you can certainly use cosmetic jewelry), build a small treasure hoard for the golden dragons. Bury or keep it somewhere special where it will not be disturbed. Ideally, the southern quadrant of your own sacred space should be used.

When your communion with the golden dragons of summer is complete, place the gratitude offering onto the burning charcoal. Speak your thanks:

Hail to the ancient and mighty dragons.
Dragons of the sacred breath,

Dragons of the sacred flame,
Dragons of the sacred water,
Dragons of the sacred earth.
We have communed with you in peace.
We have joined to you in friendship.
We heed your wisdom and guidance.
Ancient and mighty dragons,
We thank you for these mighty gifts.

If possible, allow the three dragon candles to burn down. If not, extinguish them until they can be (safely) allowed to burn completely.

FULL GOLDEN DRAGONS OF SUMMER COMMUNION RITUAL

Like the simple version, the recommended time to do this is late evening. It can be done with a group or as a solitary. It takes about one hour.

Along with the summer dragon oil and incense, you will need:

- Altar candles: Purple for spirit, gold and white for the golden dragons of summer
- Elemental dragon call: Chime or bell for quarter calls (if desired)
- Ritual fire: Lit and burning well
- Seeker candles: A small gold and white candle (for each participant)
- Incense burning container: A heat-proof container with 2–3 charcoal disks
- Offering of gratitude to the golden dragons of summer: A small bag of the summer dragon incense (for each participant). It is recommended to place the offering in tissue paper and tie it to close.

Place all of the items upon the altar. Anoint all of the tools for the ritual, including the candles, with a touch of the summer dragon oil.

Light the charcoal. When the coals are red, place a pinch of the incense onto the burning charcoal.

Light the purple spirit dragon candle and speak:

Here lies the place where the dragon dwells.
Here is an entrance to the Cavern of Crystal, Scale, and Stone.
Here gather the ancient and mighty dragons of old.

Cast the circle and call the elemental dragons, as outlined in chapter one. Stand before the altar and light the gold and white candles and speak:

Hail to the ancient and mighty dragons.
Dragons of the sacred breath,
Dragons of the sacred flame,
Dragons of the sacred waters,
Dragons of the sacred earth.
We come to you in peace.
We call to you in friendship.
We ask for your wisdom and guidance.
Ancient and mighty dragons,
We call to you!

Bow before the altar.

If this is a group ritual, give each participant a gold or white candle, rotating between gold, white, gold, and white is recommended; otherwise, take a white candle and a gold candle into each hand.

Facilitator speaks:

Welcome to the celebration of the golden dragon of summer!
Solstice celebrations have been taking place since the most
ancient of times. Bonfires were, and will be, lit to protect against
evil spirits, which some believe roam freely when the days begin to
grow short. Some even believe that dragons will be traveling in great
numbers on this day and night while on their way to gatherings
where they will celebrate the longest day of the year.

The Summer Solstice itself has remained a special moment of the
annual cycle of the year since Neolithic times. Today, we honor the
power and the might of the golden dragon, the dragon who stands
strongest when the sun reaches its pinnacle of ascension. The mighty
golden dragon, the thunder dragon, the dancing dragon of fire.

Light the white candles and speak:

Bless us with the thunder and the rain that follows.
Bless us with your knowledge.
Bless us with your secrets.
Hail to you, the golden dragon of summer!

If you have a ritual fire prepared, place the white candles around or in the
ritual fire.

Light the gold candles and speak:

Hail to the golden dragon of summer!
Storms brew, release, and then pass,
Bringing beloved rains to the earth.
Ride hard the winds and spread your wings!

Place the gold candles around or in the ritual fire.

At this point in the ritual, you can experience the golden dragon of summer meditation or share poetry, story, or song while in the sacred space.

Suggested workings:

- If you have any jewelry that can be gifted (and you can certainly use cosmetic jewelry), build a small treasure hoard for the golden dragons. Bury or keep it somewhere special where it will not be disturbed. Ideally, the southern quadrant of your own sacred space should be used.
- Take a piece of soft cloth or leather and decorate it with golden glitter. Bless the golden cloth at the altar and dedicate it to the golden dragons. Use the cloth to decorate a chosen dragon statuary, decorate a particular area of your sacred space, or burn or bury it as an offering.

After the meditation, workings, and shared poems and tales are complete, give each participant one of the small bags of incense as a gratitude offering. Hold the bags in cupped hands while still gathered around the ritual fire or burning candles.

Facilitator speaks and the participants repeat:

> *Hail to the golden dragon of summer!*
> *Bless us with the thunder and the rain that follows*
> *Bless us with your knowledge.*
> *Bless us with your secrets.*
> *Storms brew, release, and then pass,*
> *Bringing beloved rains to the earth.*
> *Ride hard the winds and spread your wings!*
> *Hail to you, the golden dragon of summer!*

Toss the gratitude offerings into the ritual fire, or burn them later if no ritual fire is being used.

> *Hail to the ancient and mighty dragons.*
> *Dragons of the sacred breath,*
> *Dragons of the sacred flame,*
> *Dragons of the sacred water,*
> *Dragons of the sacred earth.*
> *We have communed with you in peace.*
> *We have joined to you in friendship.*
> *We heed your wisdom and guidance.*
> *Ancient and mighty dragons,*
> *We thank you for these mighty gifts.*

Facilitator walks clockwise around the circle. Bow at each quarter and silently thank the elemental dragons. When back at the altar, bow again.

If possible, allow the altar candles to burn down. If not, place them in the ritual fire or extinguish them until they can be (safely) allowed to burn completely.

MEETING A GOLDEN DRAGON
OF SUMMER THROUGH MEDITATION

The golden dragons of summer teach us that through every choice we make, we initiate change. How the seeker reacts to this change and how they manage the outcome will determine whether the seeker spiritually transforms from the dragon encounter or will continue in their quest to sow the dragon's teeth. With these thoughts in mind, you can use this meditation to meet the golden dragons of summer.

The following meditation can be performed in one of the rituals or outside of ritual. If you are experiencing this meditation alone, record the meditation or have someone you trust read it to you during this communion with the dragons.

Whether alone or with a group during ritual, perform this meditation in your sacred space. Ensure that your surroundings are quiet and that you are completely comfortable (temperature, clothing choice, sitting or lying down, etc.). Make sure that this experience will not be spoiled by mundane annoyances!

Close your eyes and breathe deeply. Allow the cares and concerns of the mundane world to roll away from your neck... your shoulders... your arms... your fingers. Allow your back to relax, from your neck down, down, down, to the base of your spine ... and just breathe ....

Allow your focus to rest behind your closed eyes as you feel your body relax completely. You are still. You are quiet.

In your mind's eye, see yourself on a rocky hillside. The mighty sun is directly above you. Below you, you can see the fields that have been planted. Golden crops glisten in the sunlight. The smell of fruit that is ready for harvest is intoxicating. Everything is alive and aware. The energy of this place, of this time, is solid, good, and strong.

You stand at the bottom slope of a tall, snow-crested mountain. As you look up, you see a path that leads up the mountain.

Begin walking upon the mountain path, slowly, slowly, slowly ascending. Each footstep is deliberate and sure. Your breathing is deep and satisfying.

Take a few more steps and you will see the runestone. Take the path leading from the stone. Within a few steps, you see the entrance to the Cavern of Crystal, Scales, and Stone.

Look to the right of the cavern's entrance. There you will find a torch, lantern, or candle. Take the light and step into the cavern.

As you enter the first chamber, you sense the presence of the guardian dragon. Stop, remove your shoes, bow, and send a greeting with your name and your purpose for coming to the cavern.

Greetings, Ancient One.
I, [your name], come in peace and love, a humble seeker.

From the south, a golden mist forms and twists into the shape of a golden dragon.

Come, says the golden dragon. *Follow me.*

Follow the golden dragon through the southern cavern passage. The passage is quite warm, and the sandy floor is smooth and even. The walls are aglow with thousands of citrine crystals and yellow tiger's eye stones. The golden dragon spirit before you sways as he walks, humming a low tune that rumbles from his throat.

After a few moments, you are once again at the opening with the three passages. The golden dragon does not hesitate and enters the center passage. You follow quickly.

You emerge into a vast cavern of golden light. The brightness is that of a midday sun. There is a small creek of cool water that flows here, running north to south. The floor of the cavern is golden sand that is soft and warm upon your bare feet.

The golden dragon walks to the creek side and lies down comfortably, lowering his head to rest upon his front claws that are crossed before him.

Come, Seeker, and sit beside me, the dragon rumbles.

You go and sit beside the golden dragon. Take a moment to focus on your surroundings.

You can hear the gurgle of the creek as it winds through the cavern. The dragon beside you is still humming quietly, and you become aware of the rhythm of the song as it flows in harmony with your heartbeat…and your breath…and your own vibration.

You find yourself humming along with the golden dragon. A great joy fills you from head to toe. You feel strong. You feel confident.

> *Today is the longest of days*
> *Today we dance and sing!*
> *This day, oh! Longest of days*
> *We will crown the Summer King!*

The golden dragon's voice is inside your head, and it is a deep, gravelly voice that you join as you both sing:

> *Today is the longest of days*
> *Today we dance and sing!*
> *This day, oh! Longest of days*
> *We will crown the Summer King!*

As you sing with the dragon, you receive a vision of hundreds, even thousands, of humans celebrating the Summer Solstice. You are looking down upon the earth and see bonfires burning across the lands. The humans are dancing and feasting, from sunrise to the dark of midnight. There is much joy and hope in them on this, the longest of days.

The golden dragon then tells you to hold out your left hand and close your eyes. Your hand trembles with the energy.

Open your eyes, the golden dragon speaks to you. *Here are three dragon's teeth, seeker. You must make a choice. Will you sow the dragon's teeth? Or, will you carry them with you as you continue upon this path?*

Take some time to speak more with the golden dragon. If you wish, you may drink the cool water of the creek. Remember the smells…the sound….

The time has come to return to your own world
and your own time, the golden dragon tells you.

Take three deep breaths. Concentrate upon the back of your closed eyes. With your next breath, you feel a shift in the energy around you. You begin to feel a bit heavier as you become aware of your body.

You have returned to your safe and sacred space in this world. You feel refreshed by this communion with the dragons.

Now, one more deep breath... and open your eyes.

THE WHEEL TURNS

You have read the lore of the golden dragons of summer and had their lessons presented to you. Hopefully, your spirit is invigorated and alive with the energy of summer.

Between now and the next sabbat, take the time to meditate upon what it means to sow the dragon's teeth. Commune with the spirit of the golden dragon of summer often and remember to record your experiences into your journal

JOURNAL ENTRIES

1. Record the smells and sounds within the golden dragon's cavern.

2. Describe the three dragon's teeth.

3. Describe your choice: Did you sow the dragon's teeth or carry them with you? Record your experience.

CHAPTER EIGHT

LUGHNASADH AND THE DRAGONS OF VICTORY

Lughnasadh is the precise point between the Summer Solstice and the autumnal equinox. It is named for the Celtic god Lugh and the celebration and games competition that he held in honor of his foster mother, Tailtiu. It is also considered to be a harvest festival; for the Celts, it was the first gathering from the spring and summer crops.

This is a time of high energy that is ideal for recognizing and removing what stands between the seeker and what they truly desire from their personal journey with the dragons. Once the obstacles are revealed, the seeker will confront them and remove them. Just as the farmer reaps a bounty from the hard work of planting and tending the fields, the dragon seeker experiences and celebrates the success of their own endeavors.

The seeker will be guided through this portion of the wheel walk using the dragon lore from a Celtic myth and one of the earliest prophecies of Merlin.

LORE OF THE DRAGONS OF VICTORY

The worlds of human and dragon are very closely linked, and the energies of both influence the other. Most dragon lore focuses upon the direct interactions between the two worlds; however, there are other types of links that bind the two worlds as well.

When there is war and strife in the world of humans, that energy can seep into the dragon's abode. Similarly, when there is a conflict involving dragons in the other realms, we often sense and sometimes see the effects of that battle energy upon our own world.

The Dragons of Dinas Emrys

Deep inside a mountain in Wales, a dragon sleeps beneath a lake. At one time, there were two dragons that slept deep within the mountain; the tale of how there came to be only one comes to us from Celtic myth and the lore of Merlin and one of his earliest prophecies.

The prophecy of Merlin involves two battling dragons, but the origin of the dragon who is victorious comes from an even older tale, "Lludd and Llefelys" from the Welsh *Mabinogion*. In this lore, every May Eve, an awful screaming could be heard for miles and miles. The screech is so guttural and awful that it causes panic and chaos. The energy to create is interrupted; infertility amongst human and animal plagues the land.

Lludd eventually discovers that the screams are those of the dragon of Britain as it fights and defends its home and people. What happens next is rather bizarre at first glance: Lludd is able to subdue, capture, and confine the two battling dragons after filling them both with copious amounts of honey wine. Another side effect of the honey wine and Lludd's persuasion is that the two dragons have transformed into a creature that is quite different from their true selves: they have each become a pig. Once the "pigs" are well intoxicated, they are buried deeply within a hill that will eventually be known as Dinas Emrys.

Lludd's methods do seem strange; yet, the beguiling of dragons in order to subdue them is found in other world dragon lore. Sometimes the dragons are enchanted by magic, sometimes enticed by riddles, and on occasion, outwitted by their opponent. The plan to get the dragons drunk and then bury them deep beneath a mountain is no different, from an esoteric view, from Medea placing a spell upon the dragon of Colchis. It's simply a Celtic recipe for ridding the world of whatever is interrupting the natural order. The Greeks sought the blessings of an enchantress while the Celts preferred an overload of nature's sweet wine.

Yet, sleeping dragons can be awakened, and these two dragons certainly were. Now, we enter the time of a youthful Merlin. He is a boy, in fact, living in a village not too distant from where the dragons lie sleeping. Up on the mountain, King Vortigern is building a fortress or, rather, trying to build one. Unfortunately, every night after the day's work was done, every tower or battlement that had been built was discovered to be in a chaotic heap of rubble. It was as if the fortress was being torn apart.

Vortigern is furious and orders his wisest counselors to discover what is causing this catastrophe. After some time, Vortigern is told that the sacrifice of a "boy with no father" would satisfy the gods and allow the fortress to be completed. Off they go in search of such a lad and in quick time, they discover the young Merlin.

Merlin scoffs at the idea of his spilled blood placating the gods and settling the chaos; instead, the boy simply states that the two dragons are waking every night and battling furiously. There was a hidden pool, Merlin explained, and if it were to be drained during the day, the two dragons could be easily seen. Merlin went on to prophecy that one creature was white, and it was a Saxon dragon. The other was a red dragon, the protector and guardian of Britain. The Saxons would be defeated, the boy told the king, and the red dragon would emerge as the victory dragon.

SACRED SITE OF THE DRAGONS OF VICTORY

If ever there was a place that embodies the look and feel of a dragon's lair, it is Dinas Emrys. The "hill" rises two hundred and fifty feet above the Glaslyn river valley in Wales where there are no trees. Instead, there are rocks and boulders, and there are both in plenty. The mountain stands guard at the southern end of the Snowdon pass with a silent sentinel deep within its heart.

Dinas Emrys lies just over a mile from Beddgelert in Wales. The ruins are protected and can be easily damaged, so for access, the seeker must contact the warden in Beddgelert. A walk of just less than an hour up the northeast side of the hill will bring you up to the fort's summit.

The ruins are Iron Age and are not really the ruins of a castle; the structure is more properly called a "hillfort." Many of these structures were built in Wales (and other places) with the specific intent of guarding strategic areas. Dinas Emrys is (currently) believed to be a pre-Roman structure, but recent exploration also suggests that the structure was inhabited by the Romans during their occupation of Britain.

The site today is a small mountain covered in dense and bending trees with thousands of moss-covered rocks and boulders. The site is very much now in the embrace of its natural surroundings. Yet, as one nears the top, the trees begin to thin, and the rocks become the defining feature.

There are actually three ramparts, a few walls, and a stone foundation that are recognizable. Evidence of the pool wherein the dragons slept was also found during an excavation in the 1950s. Amazingly, during that same excavation, a platform above the pool was discovered, almost exactly as it is described in the *Historia Britainium*.[17]

There are other legends that insist Merlin lived at Dinas Emrys and even left a "golden cauldron" hidden in a cave. The treasure is meant for a particular person who will be a youth with golden hair and blue eyes. When he or she approaches the spot where the cauldron is hidden, a bell will ring and the protective barrier around the treasure will crumble.

---

17. William John Gruffydd, *Folklore and Myth in the Mabinogion: A Lecture Delivered at the National Museum of Wales on 27 October 1950* (New York: Read Books, 2013), n. p.

This site is not terribly busy; but, as stated before, the seeker should contact the warden before climbing the hill. The western slope is very dangerous and should not be traversed at all. Once you have reached the top, it is usually fairly quiet and tranquil. Here, amongst the aged stones, it is truly effortless to gaze upon the magnificent mountains of Wales and commune with the spirits of the dragons of victory in this amazing place.

COMMUNING WITH THE DRAGONS OF VICTORY ON LUGHNASADH

The victory dragons for this particular working are adorned with silver scales that are tinged with red and white. The energy and excitement of being a champion surrounds victory dragons. They are high-energy creatures that bring satisfaction and reward. As with the previous dragons, you can commune with these dragons through the following simple or complex rituals as well as through a stand-alone meditation. These rituals are intended to celebrate both the dragons of victory and empower the seeker's journey in search of the them.

DRAGONS OF VICTORY RITUAL OIL AND INCENSE

Before either ritual, you will need to prepare the necessary oil and incense.

First, prepare the victorious dragon oil. You will need:

- 2 tablespoons consecrated frankincense oil
- 7 drops consecrated dragon's blood oil
- 5 drops consecrated patchouli oil
- 3 drops consecrated sandalwood oil
- 1 drop consecrated water
- 3 breaths (yours) upon the mixed oils
- 9 drops of consecrated cedar

Take the oils and water and combine to make the victorious dragon oil. Once the oils and water are combined in a container, hold the container in your left hand. Outstretch your right hand and hold over the bowl; speak these words:

I declare this oil as sacred to my purpose.

Pause for three breaths. Then speak the chant:

Hail to the ancestors.
We honor your sacrifice.
We honor your wisdom.

Next, prepare the victorious dragon incense. You will need:

- 2 tablespoons of dragon's blood resin
- ⅓ teaspoon of patchouli
- ⅓ teaspoon of frankincense
- ⅓ teaspoon of copal
- ⅓ teaspoon of cedar

Take the ingredients and combine in a container to make the dragon of victory incense. Once combined, hold the container in your left hand. Outstretch your right hand and hold over the bowl; speak these words:

I declare this incense as sacred to my purpose.

SIMPLE DRAGONS OF VICTORY COMMUNION RITUAL

The recommended time to do this is late evening. It takes about one hour. Along with the prepared victorious dragon oil and incense, you will need:

- Dragon candles (3): Purple for spirit, red and white candles for the dragons of victory

- Incense burning container: A heat-proof container with 2–3 charcoal disks

- Offering of gratitude to the dragons of victory: A small bag of the victorious dragon incense. It is recommended to place the offering in tissue paper and tie it to close.

Light the charcoal. When the coals are red, place a pinch of the incense onto the burning charcoal.

Light the purple spirit dragon candle and speak:

> *Here lies the place where the dragon dwells.*
> *Here is an entrance to the Cavern of Crystal, Scale, and Stone.*
> *Here gather the ancient and mighty dragons of old.*

Light the red and white dragons of victory candles and speak:

> *Hail to the ancient and mighty dragons.*
> *Dragons of the sacred breath,*
> *Dragons of the sacred flame,*
> *Dragons of the sacred water,*
> *Dragons of the sacred earth.*
> *We come to you in peace.*
> *We call to you in friendship.*
> *We ask for your wisdom and guidance.*
> *Ancient and mighty dragons,*
> *We call to you!*

Now, you are ready to experience the dragons of victory meditation. When you have completed the meditation, write down your journal entries.

When your communion with the dragons of victory is complete, place the gratitude offering onto the burning charcoal. Speak your thanks:

> *Hail to the ancient and mighty dragons.*
> *Dragons of the sacred breath,*

Dragons of the sacred flame,
Dragons of the sacred water,
Dragons of the sacred earth.
We have communed with you in peace.
We have joined to you in friendship.
We heed your wisdom and guidance.
Ancient and mighty dragons,
We thank you for these mighty gifts.

If possible, allow the three dragon candles to burn down. If not, extinguish them until they can be (safely) allowed to burn completely.

FULL DRAGONS OF VICTORY COMMUNION RITUAL

Like the simple version, the recommended time to do this is late evening. It can be done with a group or as a solitary. It takes about one hour.

Along with the victorious dragon oil and incense, you will need:

- Altar candles: Purple for spirit, red and white for the dragons of victory
- Elemental dragon call: Chime or bell for quarter calls (if desired)
- Ritual fire: Lit and burning well
- Seeker candles: A small red and white candle (for each participant)
- Incense burning container: A heat-proof container with 2–3 charcoal disks
- Offering of gratitude to the dragons of victory: A small bag of the victorious dragon incense (for each participant). It is recommended to place the offering in tissue paper and tie it to close.

Place all of the items upon the altar. Anoint all of the tools for the ritual, including the candles, with a touch of the victorious dragon oil.

Light the charcoal. When the coals are red, place a pinch of the incense onto the burning charcoal.

Light the purple spirit dragon candle (upon the altar) and speak:

Here lies the place where the dragon dwells.
Here is an entrance to the Cavern of Crystal, Scales, and Stone.
Here gather the ancient and mighty dragons of old.

Cast the circle and call the elemental dragons, as outlined in chapter one. Stand before the altar and light the red and white candles and speak:

Hail to the ancient and mighty dragons.
Dragons of the sacred breath,
Dragons of the sacred flame,
Dragons of the sacred waters,
Dragons of the sacred earth.
We come to you in peace.
We call to you in friendship.
We ask for your wisdom and guidance.
Ancient and mighty dragons,
We call to you!

Bow before the altar.

If this is a group ritual, give each participant a red or white candle, rotating between red, white, red, and white is recommended; otherwise, take a red candle and a white candle into each hand.

Facilitator speaks:

Welcome to our celebration of the victory dragons! This day is
often celebrated with grains that have been harvested and
made into bread. Competitions and games are played
where the victor is hailed as both hero and champion.
Today, we honor the power and the might of the victory
dragons, the dragons who aid us in achieving victory.
The spirits that aid us in reaching our goals.

Light the small red candles and speak:

Bless us with victory.
Bless us with strength.
Let us see what chains us.
Let us find the key to those chains.
Hail to you, dragons of victory!

If you have a ritual fire prepared, light the ritual fire and place the red candles around or in the ritual fire.

Light the white candles and speak:

Hail to the victory dragons!
Let us be champions of our own destiny.
A pride of dragons comes with storm clouds and wind.
Fly high and spread your wings!

Place the white candles around or in the ritual fire.

At this point in the ritual, you can experience the victory dragon meditation or share poetry, story, or song while in the sacred space.

Suggested workings:

- Take four plates of fresh breads and grains, bless them at the altar, and then go to each quarter of the circle and leave a plate for each of the Elemental guardian dragons. Similarly, take four vessels of beer, bless at the altar, and leave one vessel at each of the quarters.
- Have a basket of breads and grains blessed at the altar. Eat the bread as part of your sacred feast or post-ritual feast and use the blessed grains for your next growing season.
- Acknowledge the participants in the circle who have achieved victory, in whatever form it has manifested. Celebrate the defeat of an illness or the triumph of a champion.

After the meditation, workings, and shared poems and tales are complete, give each participant one of the small bags of incense as a gratitude offering.

Hold the bags in cupped hands while still gathered around the ritual fire or burning candles.

Facilitator speaks and the participants repeat:

> *Hail to the victory dragons!*
> *A pride of dragons comes with storm clouds and wind.*
> *Fly high and spread your wings!*
> *Let us see what chains us.*
> *Let us find the key to those chains.*
> *Hail to you, the dragons of victory!*

Toss the gratitude offerings into the ritual fire, or burn them later if no ritual fire is being used.

Return to the altar and speak:

> *Hail to the ancient and mighty dragons.*
> *Dragons of the sacred breath,*
> *Dragons of the sacred flame,*
> *Dragons of the sacred waters,*
> *Dragons of the sacred earth.*
> *We come to you in peace.*
> *We call to you in friendship.*
> *We ask for your wisdom and guidance.*
> *Ancient and mighty dragons,*
> *We thank you for these mighty gifts.*

Facilitator walks clockwise around the circle. Bow at each quarter and silently thank the elemental dragons. When back at the altar, bow again.

If possible, allow the altar candles to burn down. If not, place them in the ritual fire or extinguish them until they can be (safely) allowed to burn completely.

MEETING A DRAGON OF
VICTORY THROUGH MEDITATION

The dragons of victory enable the seeker to recognize what is blocking their progression upon this path. They teach us that for every obstacle, there is a solution. How the seeker removes the obstacles, whether through clever subterfuge or outright battle, will determine the next steps for the wheel walk. With these thoughts in mind, you are ready to meet the spirit of a victory dragon.

The following meditation can be performed in one of the rituals or outside of ritual. If you are experiencing this meditation alone, record the meditation or have someone you trust read it to you during this communion with the dragons.

Whether alone or with a group during ritual, perform this meditation in your sacred space. Ensure that your surroundings are quiet and that you are completely comfortable (temperature, clothing choice, sitting or lying down, etc.). Make sure that this experience will not be spoiled by mundane annoyances!

Close your eyes and breathe deeply. Allow the cares and concerns of the mundane world to roll away from your neck ... your shoulders ... your arms ... your fingers. Allow your back to relax, from your neck down, down, down, to the base of your spine ... and just breathe ....

Allow your focus to rest behind your closed eyes as you feel your body relax completely. You are still. You are quiet.

In your mind's eye, see yourself on a rocky hillside. It is late afternoon. The sun has begun its descent to the western horizon. Yet, the world is bathed in the warmth of summer. The energy of this place, of this time, is solid, good, and strong.

You stand at the bottom slope of a tall, snow-crested mountain. As you look up, you see a path that leads up the mountain.

Begin walking upon the mountain path, slowly, slowly, slowly ascending. Each footstep is deliberate and sure. Your breathing is deep and satisfying.

Take a few more steps and you will see the runestone. Take the path leading from the stone. Within a few steps, you see the entrance to the Cavern of Crystal, Scales, and Stone.

Look to the right of the cavern's entrance. There you will find a torch, lantern, or candle. Take the light and step into the cavern.

As you enter the first chamber, you sense the presence of the guardian dragon. Stop, remove your shoes, bow, and send a greeting with your name and your purpose for coming to the cavern.

> *Greetings, Ancient One.*
> *I, [your name], come in peace and love, a humble seeker.*

A red mist forms and twists, then divides to form into the shapes of three victory dragons.

> *Come,* they say in unison. *Follow us.*

Follow the dragons of victory through the Southern cavern passage. The passage is very warm, and the sandy floor is smooth and even. The walls are aglow with thousands of rubies, white opals, and garnets. The victory dragons move smoothly ahead of you. Their scales make a tinkling sound as they move, rather like tiny bells ringing in the distance. The sound is soothing and exciting.

After a few moments, you are once again at the opening with the three passages. The victory dragons enter the right passage. You follow.

You emerge into a vast cavern that is aglow with a hundred bonfires. As you follow the victory dragons to the center of the cavern, you notice hundreds of shadows running and jumping around the bonfires. From far, far away, you can hear the cheering and shouts of humans.

> *The games have commenced,* speaks one of the dragons
> as he stares into the largest of the bonfires.

See the reflection of the flames in the dragons' eyes as they stare into the fire.

> *Place the resin upon the coals there at the edge of*
> *the flames,* the dragon on the left instructs you.

Suddenly, in your right hand, there is a small amount of a sticky, sweet-smelling resin. Frankincense.

> *At the edge,* says the dragon on the right,
> *put the resin on the coals. Then, sit and see.*

You gently toss the frankincense upon the coals and then sit nearby. The sweet aroma of the resin relaxes you. As the smoke from the frankincense rises and silhouettes against the hot, orange flames, you begin to see images forming....

> *Flames become wings*
> *Wood becomes bone*
> *Within the flames you see a mountain crested with fire*
> *Always burning*
> *Within the mountain, you now know that the dragons are born*

You see an enormous red dragon rise from the mountain. It spreads its wings and screams a battle cry. A white dragon swoops from the sky, and the two dragons begin to battle. Twisting through the air, the dragons bite and claw, each grappling for an advantage. As they begin to descend towards the ground, the red dragon rips away one of the white dragon's wings. The dragons disengage. The red dragon rises triumphantly while the white dragon plunges into the mountain.

Silence follows. Your focus shifts to the area below the mountain.

Far below, in fields of gold, you see humans gathering the grains of summer. Mothers form the grains into bread, and the bread is blessed. Fathers form the grains into hearty beer, and the beer is blessed.

Everywhere, every human stands around a sacred bonfire, a horn of beer in their right hand and a torn piece of blessed bread in their left. In unison, the humans cheer and pray to the old gods.

> *Let us join them,* the three victory dragons speak.

There, in your right hand, is a cool and hearty draught of beer. In your left, is warm, fresh bread. Looking at the dragons, they also have the fruits of the sacred harvest.

> *May the grains that have been blessed by the*
> *gods sustain us,* says the center dragon.
> *May the grains that have been blessed by the*
> *gods enrich us,* says the dragon on the right.
> *May the grains that have been blessed by the*
> *gods empower us,* says the dragon on the left.
> *Let us celebrate our victories and share our rewards!*
> all three dragons say in harmony.

You drink your mug of beer, leaving a small amount as an offering to the gods. You taste the bread, again leaving a small amount as an offering to the gods.

Take some time to speak more with the dragons of victory.

Remember the smells … the sounds ….

> *The time has come to return to your own world*
> *and your own time,* the dragons tell you.

Take three deep breaths. Concentrate upon the back of your closed eyes. With your next breath, you feel a shift in the energy around you. You begin to feel a bit heavier as you become aware of your body.

You have returned to your safe and sacred space in this world. You feel refreshed by this communion with the dragons.

Now, one more deep breath … and open your eyes.

THE WHEEL TURNS

Your spirit should be strong with a sense of triumph after your communion and celebration with the dragons of victory. You are ready to carry this energy forward until the next sabbat at the autumnal equinox. Remember, this is a period of high energy that is ideal for recognizing and removing what stands between you and what you truly desire to achieve from your communion with the dragons.

For the next six weeks, work to identify these obstacles. Record them. Meditate upon them. Then through meditation and time in sacred space, investigate and confront these barriers. When the wheel turns towards the autumnal equinox, you will be poised to harvest the dragon's bounty.

JOURNAL ENTRIES

1. Record an interpretation for the dragons' words. What are the dragons trying to convey to you?

2. Describe your vision of the battling dragons. Record any smells, sounds, or feelings that you experienced.

3. Describe your vision of the three victory dragons.

CHAPTER NINE

AUTUMNAL EQUINOX AND THE HARVEST DRAGONS

The autumnal equinox is a time when the world is in perfect balance. This is a harvest festival. From this day forward, the world will grow colder, and the land will slowly drift into its winter slumber.

The energy for this time is smooth and quiet; yet, there is an edge of anticipation as well. This portion of the wheel walk will focus upon the cycle of life, death, and rebirth. These are uncomfortable transitions and some-times even painful; yet, this type of growth also has the potential for yielding great rewards. This cycle is followed by all life here on our planet. We plant, we coax growth, and then we harvest.

LORE OF THE HARVEST DRAGONS

The realm of the harvest dragon is grounded in rich soil, clear waters, and falling leaves. These dragons are guardians of their realms. Their stories are lessons of loyalty and sacrifice.

At this point on the wheel, the seeker will be guided to harvest the bounty from their personal projects. Through story, ritual, and meditation, the seeker will be introduced to the energy of the harvest dragons.

The Ismenian Dragon

In ancient Greece, in the land of Boeotia, a dragon dutifully guarded a sacred spring that was named for the Greek nymph Ismene. The dragon was the offspring of the mighty god of war, Ares. For years, probably centuries, the dragon had guarded the sacred site and only allowed the water to be used for either washing or drinking by those who he deemed worthy. The dragon lived in a cave nearby. He came to be known as the *Drakon Ismenios*, or the Ismenian Dragon.

The Ismenian Dragon was a guardian dragon who was tasked by the gods to guard a sacred spring. Like most Greek dragons, this creature was enormous. In *Metamorphoses,* Ovid describes the dragon as able to raise its head above the highest tree that grew near the spring. In addition to being the offspring of a god, the dragon possessed deadly venom, three rows of teeth, and a forked tongue.[18]

The energy of this dragon, like all guardians, is protective and defensive. It is watchful and completely aware of everything in its domain. It deems who is worthy of drinking or washing with the sacred waters; it is the *dragon's* judgement that determines who will receive the blessings from the energy of the place.

The dragon's fate is intertwined with that of the Greek hero Cadmus. When Cadmus's journey intersects with that of the dragon, it is a time for

---

18. Ovid, "Book 3" in *Metamorphoses* (New York: Penguin Classics, 2004), n. p.

the dragon to transform. This loyal dragon will not simply "die" and be forgotten; he will be the catalyst for a new kingdom. His sacrifice will birth a new nation. Out of the chaos of a blood-soaked field of battle, a proud city and culture will be born. The guardian thus becomes the seed for creation.

Cadmus was a young man who was searching for his lost sister, Europa. Cadmus had visited the mighty Oracle at Delphi and been told to abandon his search; instead, the god Apollo wished for him to build a new city. The Oracle told Cadmus to follow a cow that had not yet been yoked until it stopped. At that spot, he should build the city.

Cadmus did as the Oracle had advised; when the spot had been "chosen" by the cow, Cadmus built an altar to Jove. He sent several of his traveling companions to a nearby well to get water as he prepared a sacrifice for the goddess. As fate would have it, the nearby well was the spring of Ismene, guarded by the Ismenian Dragon, son of Ares.

Cadmus's companions were very quickly slain by the dragon. When Cadmus missed them and went to see what had delayed the gathering of the water, he found them dead. Angry, Cadmus avenged his comrades by slaying the Ismenian Dragon. He then took the water and made his offering to the goddess.

Athena was apparently pleased, but she advised Cadmus to do a very strange thing: take the teeth of the slain dragon and sow them on the nearby ground. Dutifully, not unlike the dragon that he had slain, Cadmus ploughed the ground, and the dragon's teeth were planted as Athena had directed.

It did not take long for Cadmus's crop of dragon's teeth to produce a miraculous harvest: from the dragon's teeth came full-grown, mighty warriors, the *Spartoi*, sons of the dragon's teeth. These were full-grown offspring of Ares, fully armed and ready for battle.

Cadmus looked on the field of warriors in amazement and a little fear. These were formidable warriors whom he alone could not defeat. However, the goddess Athena intervened again by handing Cadmus a single stone. Cadmus was not sure how a small rock could be a weapon against so many. Still, Athena told him to throw it at one of the sons of the dragon's teeth and then watch.

Cadmus did as the goddess instructed and struck one of the warriors in the head with the stone. The Son of Ares became furious and began to madly fight his brothers. A rousing battle ensued that resulted in a blood-soaked field of human corpses.

The sons of the dragon's teeth fought until the sun set. When the day was done, only five remained. The goddess advised Cadmus to now speak to the warriors and bargain with them to stop fighting amongst themselves. She wanted Cadmus to invite them to join him in founding a new city, which would be called Thebes. The warriors agreed.

All appeared to be well. Even the god Ares seemed to forgive Cadmus for slaying his dragon and for outwitting his sons of the dragon's teeth. The god of war made peace with Cadmus by offering his daughter, Harmonia, to be the new king's bride. Thus, the great kingdom of Thebes was founded.

Years later, Cadmus and Harmonia left Thebes. As Cadmus and Harmonia wandered the lands, the old king could not escape a burden that weighed heavily upon his mind. He wondered if his discontent and inability to feel joy was because, all those years ago, he had slain the Ismenian Dragon.

Cadmus finally voiced this concern, saying that if indeed the dragon's death had somehow cursed him, then he wished to spend the remainder of his life as a dragon. Instantly, the former king of Thebes and his wife were transformed into small serpents. For Cadmus, the journey began anew. This time, though, *he* was the dragon.[19]

Sons of the Dragon's Teeth

On this wheel walk, the dragon seeker will encounter the sons of the dragon's teeth in two pieces of dragon lore: *Cadmus and the Founding of Thebes* and in *Jason and the Argonauts* (see chapter seven). The slain dragon clearly still possesses very potent dragon energy. The dragon's remains are used to empower and invoke the pattern of life, death, and rebirth. The seeker learns that *from chaos comes creation.*

In our time, "sowing the dragon's teeth" has become a metaphor that is commonly used to describe when someone or something has taken action

---

19. Ovid, "Book 4" in *Metamorphoses*, n. p.

that leads to conflict. Of course, as we can see from the dragon lore, the conflict and chaos are just the beginning of a journey that is constantly rebirthed. As magickal practitioners, our lesson is that we should look beyond the beginning chaos with the wisdom that this untamed energy is part of the dragon's creation cycle. Once we learn to recognize this pattern of dragon energy, it becomes our responsibility to allow and, on occasion, ensure that the cycle continues uninterrupted.

The Dragon of Delphi

During the time of the Titans, the Temple and Oracle of Delphi were under the protection of Gaia. Gaia's chosen guardian was an enormous dragon. This was an ancient dragon believed to have been born from the muddy and slimy waters of the ancient world. The dragon lived in a cave in Mount Parnassus and had the ability to become invisible.

It was Apollo, son of Zeus, who was fated to slay the creature. In some lore, Apollo is avenging his mother's death; in other tales, he is allegedly saving the world from the dragon's mischief and woe. Whatever his reason, the young Apollo, even armed with a bow and arrow forged by Hephaestus himself, was facing a formidable task.

He attacked the dragon with an onslaught of arrows. When the one-hundredth arrow struck the dragon, the dragon was slain. Apollo claimed the shrine and left the rotting corpse of the dragon outside of the main Delphic temple.

Gaia, and others, were not too terribly pleased with Apollo's actions. The shrine, with the dragon's remains left for all to see, continued to serve the ancient world as a site for pilgrimage and enlightenment.

SACRED SITES OF THE HARVEST DRAGONS

Oracle of Delphi

The Temple of Apollo in Delphi, Greece, is one of the most ancient and famous sacred sites in the entire world. The shrine has been known to the civilized world since the seventh century BCE. The Oracle delivered prophecies until 393 CE, when Emperor Theodosius I ordered the Pagan temples to cease their active worship.

The shrine sits on the southwestern slope of Mount Parnassus. It was considered by the classical world to be the *center* of the known world. This is where the omphalos, a stone that represented the "navel" of the world, was kept. Once also called Pytho, Delphi is where the High Priestess of the Temple of Apollo would speak the prophecies that literally moved humans and nations in the ancient world. In the Hellenic world, the oracle prophesied to all who could make the pilgrimage and wait for their turn with the priestess. Commoners, aristocracy, and royalty came from far and wide to hear her words.

Delphi is one of the few ancient Pagan sacred sites that has not been built upon or somehow transformed from its original intent. The ruins are there today located at the corner of what is now called Holy Street and Temple Street.

Today, millions of people visit Greece each year, and the Delphi site is a frequent stop. There may not be an active oracle providing prophecies, but the site is still considered sacred and is cared for as such.

Sacred Spring of Ismene

In ancient Greece, the sacred springs were believed to be sites where the world of the gods opened and intersected with the world of humans. The springs were used for cleansing one's self, physically and spiritually, before entering a nearby temple or altar. In many places, the priests, oracles, and worshippers all used the same sacred spring to prepare for their communion with the gods.

These dragons were completely dedicated and loyal to their set purpose: only allow the "worthy" to approach and be blessed by the water.

Metaphysically, these dragons hold the tension, even *become* the tension, that exists when the world of the gods hovers near the world of humans. They embody the vortex energy that exists near the crossing of ley lines. They are not just simple "guard dogs" with teeth and venom; they must use their entire being to *allow* the communion between the gods and humans. Yet, as we have seen, there does come a time when the dragon must transform and even sacrifice its life. The only thing constant is change.

The modern-day "city" of Thebes is a small market town that is now called Thiva. The sites associated with Cadmus's dragon lore are in ruins;

in fact, the sacred spring of Ismene's exact location is unknown to modern humans. Still, there is a site called *Ismenios Folos* that is located just a short distance from the ruins of the Cadmea. Today, the hill is vibrantly green and one of the few areas of Thiva that has not been built upon. Sadly, no water flows there now, but it was obviously once a place from which an underground spring flowed into a nearby collecting pool.

There is no modern formal worship at the site, and it is quite tucked away and easy to miss. Yet, here once existed a gateway to the world of the gods. It was here that worshippers once prepared for their communion with the gods under the watchful eye of a guardian dragon.

COMMUNING WITH THE HARVEST DRAGONS ON THE AUTUMNAL EQUINOX

The harvest dragon's energies aid us in effectively harvesting what we have sown both literally and metaphysically. It is during this time of the wheel walk that we are able to see the fruits of our labors. If we have been wise, honored the gods, and maintained harmony, we will see that the seed has transformed into bounty. As with the previous dragons, you can commune with the harvest dragons through the following simple or complex rituals as well as through a stand-alone meditation.

These rituals are intended to honor not only those who gather the harvest, but also to the sacrifices that make the harvest possible. Transformation is inevitable and often uncomfortable; still, with proper preparation and wisdom, change can bring forth powerful and wonderful things for the seeker.

HARVEST DRAGON RITUAL OIL AND INCENSE

Before either ritual, you will need to prepare the necessary oil and incense.

First, prepare the harvest dragon oil. You will need:

- 2 tablespoons consecrated frankincense oil
- 7 drops consecrated dragon's blood oil

- 5 drops consecrated patchouli oil
- 3 drops consecrated sandalwood oil
- 1 drop consecrated water
- 3 breaths (yours) upon the mixed oils
- 9 drops of consecrated cypress oil

Take the oils and water and combine to make the harvest dragon oil. Once the oils and water are combined in a container, hold the container in your left hand. Outstretch your right hand and hold over the bowl; speak these words:

I declare this oil as sacred to my purpose.

Pause for three breaths. Then speak the chant:

Hail to the ones who gather,
We call you to join us for this harvest.
We ask you to bless the grains.
We ask you to bless the herds.
Hail to you, dragons of the harvest.

Next, prepare the harvest dragon incense. You will need:

- 2 tablespoons of dragon's blood resin
- ⅓ teaspoon of patchouli
- ⅓ teaspoon of frankincense
- ⅓ teaspoon of copal
- ⅓ teaspoon of cypress

Take the ingredients and combine in a container to make the harvest dragon incense. Once combined, hold the container in your left hand. Outstretch your right hand and hold over the bowl; speak these words:

I declare this incense as sacred to my purpose.

SIMPLE HARVEST DRAGON COMMUNION RITUAL

The recommended time to do this is late evening. It takes about one hour. Along with the prepared harvest dragon oil and incense, you will need:

- Dragon candles (3): Purple for spirit, gold and brown candles for the harvest dragons
- Incense burning container: A heat-proof container with 2–3 charcoal disks
- Offering of gratitude to the harvest dragons: A small bag of the harvest dragon incense. It is recommended to place the offering in tissue paper and tie it to close.

Light the charcoal. When the coals are red, place a pinch of the incense onto the burning charcoal.

Light the purple spirit dragon candle and speak:

Here lies the place where the dragon dwells.
Here is an entrance to the Cavern of Crystal, Scale, and Stone.
Here gather the ancient and mighty dragons of old.

Light the gold and brown harvest dragon candles and speak:

Hail to the ancient and mighty dragons.
Dragons of the sacred breath,
Dragons of the sacred flame,
Dragons of the sacred water,
Dragons of the sacred earth.
We come to you in peace.
We call to you in friendship.
We ask for your wisdom and guidance.
Ancient and mighty dragons,
We call to you!

Now, you are ready to experience the harvest dragon meditation. When you have completed the meditation, write down your journal entries.

When your communion with the harvest dragon is complete, place the gratitude offering onto the burning charcoal. Speak your thanks:

> *Hail to the ancient and mighty dragons.*
> *Dragons of the sacred breath,*
> *Dragons of the sacred flame,*
> *Dragons of the sacred water,*
> *Dragons of the sacred earth.*
> *We have communed with you in peace.*
> *We have joined to you in friendship.*
> *We heed your wisdom and guidance.*
> *Ancient and mighty dragons,*
> *We thank you for these mighty gifts.*

If possible, allow the three dragon candles to burn down. If not, extinguish them until they can be (safely) allowed to burn completely.

FULL HARVEST DRAGON COMMUNION RITUAL

Like the simple version, the recommended time to do this is late evening. It can be done with a group or as a solitary. It takes about one hour.

Along with the harvest dragon oil and incense, you will need:

- Altar candles: Purple for spirit, gold and brown for the harvest dragons
- Elemental dragon call: Chime or bell for quarter calls (if desired)
- Ritual fire: Prepared for lighting
- Seeker candles: A small gold and brown candle (for each participant)
- Incense burning container: A heat-proof container with 2–3 charcoal disks
- Offering of gratitude to the harvest dragons: A small bag of the harvest dragon incense, (for each participant). It is recommended to place the offering in tissue paper and tie it to close.

Place all of the items upon the altar. Anoint all of the tools for the ritual, including the candles, with a touch of the harvest dragon oil.

Light the charcoal. When the coals are red, place a pinch of the incense onto the burning charcoal.

Light the purple spirit dragon candle (upon the altar) and speak:

Here lies the place where the dragon dwells.
Here is an entrance to the Cavern of Crystal, Scales, and Stone.
Here gather the ancient and mighty dragons of old.

Cast the circle and call the elemental dragons, as outlined in chapter one. Stand before the altar and light the gold and brown candles and speak:

Hail to the ancient and mighty dragons.
Dragons of the sacred breath,
Dragons of the sacred flame,
Dragons of the sacred waters,
Dragons of the sacred earth.
We come to you in peace.
We call to you in friendship.
We ask for your wisdom and guidance.
Ancient and mighty dragons,
We call to you!

Bow before the altar.

If this is a group ritual, give each participant a small gold candle and a brown candle; otherwise, take a gold candle and a brown candle into each hand.

Facilitator speaks:

Welcome to our celebration of the harvest dragon! In the fields,
the farmers will start to bring in their crops. The herds are
prepared for the annual culling. For everyone, we can now
begin to reap the harvest of our hopes and dreams.

Today, we honor the power and the might of the harvest dragons,
the dragons who aid us in gathering our spiritual harvest.

Light the gold candles and speak:

Hail to the Ones who gather,
We call you to join us for this harvest.
We ask you to bless the grains.
We ask you to bless the herds.
Hail to you, dragons of the harvest.

If you have a ritual fire prepared, light the ritual fire and place the gold candles around or in the ritual fire.

Light the brown candles and speak:

Hail to the harvest dragons!
Let us be the sowers of change.
Let us be the gatherers of bounty.
Let us dance smoothly with the rhythms of the land.

Place the brown candles around or in the ritual fire.

At this point in the ritual, you can experience the harvest dragon meditation or share poetry, story, or song while in the sacred space.

Suggested workings:

- Place some of your harvest upon the altar or create a special harvest altar for this ritual. The "harvest" could be actual crops or the "fruits" of any labor from the prior growing season. Formally thank the gods for the harvest and offer the altar and the items upon it as thanks.

- If in a group setting, have participants share their individual "harvest experiences."

After the meditation or working is complete, give each participant a bag of incense. Hold the bags in cupped hands while still gathered around the ritual fire or burning candles.

Facilitator speaks and the participants repeat:

> *Hail to the harvest dragon!*
> *Fly high and spread your wings!*
> *We call you to join us for this harvest.*
> *We ask you to bless the grains.*
> *We ask you to bless the herds.*
> *Hail to you, the harvest dragon!*

Toss the gratitude offerings into the ritual fire, or burn them later if no ritual fire is being used.

Return to the altar and speak:

> *Hail to the ancient and mighty dragons.*
> *Dragons of the sacred breath,*
> *Dragons of the sacred flame,*
> *Dragons of the sacred waters,*
> *Dragons of the sacred earth.*
> *We have communed with you in peace.*
> *We have joined to you in friendship.*
> *We heed your wisdom and guidance.*
> *Ancient and mighty dragons,*
> *We thank you for these mighty gifts.*

Facilitator walks clockwise around the circle. Bow at each quarter and silently thank the elemental dragons. When back at the altar, bow again.

If possible, allow the altar candles to burn down. If not, place them in the ritual fire or extinguish them until they can be (safely) allowed to burn completely.

MEETING A HARVEST DRAGON
THROUGH MEDITATION

The harvest dragons are our partners for gathering what we have planted upon our spiritual path. We honor both the harvest of our journey along with the sacrifices that we have made. You have been shown that change is inevitable and oftentimes uncomfortable. With these thoughts in mind, it is time to meet the spirit of a harvest dragon.

The following meditation can be performed in one of the rituals or outside of ritual. If you are experiencing this meditation alone, record the meditation or have someone you trust read it to you during this communion with the dragons.

Whether alone or with a group during ritual, perform this meditation in your sacred space. Ensure that your surroundings are quiet and that you are completely comfortable (temperature, clothing choice, sitting or lying down, etc.). Make sure that this experience will not be spoiled by mundane annoyances!

Close your eyes and breathe deeply. Allow the cares and concerns of the mundane world to roll away from your neck … your shoulders … your arms … your fingers. Allow your back to relax, from your neck down, down, down, to the base of your spine … and just breathe ….

Allow your focus to rest behind your closed eyes as you feel your body relax completely. You are still. You are quiet.

In your mind's eye, see yourself on a rocky hillside. The leaves of the trees are now glorious reds and golds. The flowers are retreating and preparing for their winter's rest. The air is chilled but not unpleasant. The energy of this place, of this time, is solid, good, and strong.

You stand at the bottom slope of a tall, snow-crested mountain. As you look up, you see a path that leads up the mountain. The sun is setting in the west; the sky is swirling with red, orange, yellow. The air is crisp and becoming cooler with each breath.

Begin walking upon the mountain path, slowly, slowly, slowly ascending. Each footstep is deliberate and sure. Your breathing is deep and satisfying.

Take a few more steps and you will see the runestone. Take the path leading from the stone. Within a few steps, you see the entrance to the Cavern of Crystal, Scales, and Stone.

Look to the right of the cavern's entrance. There you will find a torch, lantern, or candle. Take the light and step into the cavern.

As you enter the first chamber, you sense the presence of the guardian dragon. Stop, remove your shoes, bow, and send a greeting with your name and your purpose for coming to the cavern.

Greetings, Ancient One.
I, [your name], come in peace and love, a humble seeker.

A gold, brownish mist forms into the shape of the harvest dragon.

Come, the dragon says quietly.

Follow the harvest dragon through the western cavern passage. The passage is pleasantly cool, and the floor is of polished stone. The walls are aglow with thousands of citrine crystals. The harvest dragon walks ahead of you in silence.

After a few moments, you stand at the opening of three passages. The harvest dragon enters the left passage. You follow.

The cavern is lit by hundreds of torches, and you can see row upon row of crops ready to be taken: corn, peas, beans, and wheat.

Take this basket, says the harvest dragon.

The dragon hands you a large woven basket. Take the basket in your hands.

Now, gather what you have sown.

The dragon nods at you then towards the field of crops.

Now, go.

Walk to the first row of the field, which happens to be a row of corn. Grab an ear of corn, pull it from the stalk, and then toss it into your basket.

Continue to pull the ears of corn. When you finish the row of corn, move to the next row of crop. Soon, as you continue to harvest, the basket becomes full. You walk back to where the harvest dragon stands.

> *Good. Now your basket is full. Well done. What, though,*
> *shall we do with the rest of the crop?* speaks the dragon.

Surely, there will be others who also should partake of this harvest? Should you harvest it all and store some for later? Or, allow others to come and share in the harvest?

> *Shall we leave it or harvest it?* asks the dragon.

Make your decision to either continue your harvest or leave it for others to reap.

> *Now we will give thanks for this bounty,* says the harvest dragon.
> *Take half of your full harvest and place it on the floor here.*

The harvest dragon nods to a large, white rock in the floor.
Take your basket to the rock and carefully select what you will give and what you will keep.
Remember the smells … the sounds ….

> *The time has come to return to your own world*
> *and your own time,* the dragons tell you.

Take three deep breaths. Concentrate upon the back of your closed eyes. With your next breath, you feel a shift in the energy around you. You begin to feel a bit heavier as you become aware of your body.

You have returned to your safe and sacred space in this world. You feel refreshed by this communion with the dragons.

Now, one more deep breath … and open your eyes.

THE WHEEL TURNS

Now that you have met the spirit of the harvest dragon, take the time between now and the next sabbat to deeply reflect upon that experience. The meditation is a vision of gathering your personal harvest; however, you may find other messages that are unique to your experience.

Commune with the spirit of the harvest dragon as often as you can. Use the meditation or simple quiet time in sacred space. Always have your journal close by to document each visit to the cavern as well as any insights that may come to you.

JOURNAL ENTRIES

1. Did you harvest all of the growing crop or leave it for others?

2. Describe the feel and smell of the fresh crops.

3. Describe your vision of the harvest dragon.

CONCLUSION

THE JOURNEY
BEGINS ANEW

Your wheel walk with the magickal dragons is drawing to a conclusion. Yet, if you have learned anything from our wheel walk with the dragons, then you know that this "end" is simply the pause before you begin again.

The dragon seeker has communed with the ancestor dragons and seen the creation of the world. The ice dragons have shown you the power of transformation from their own sacrifice. The waking dragons taught the seeker that seeing *and* being "unseen" are equally important to spiritual evolution. The dragons of making empowered the seeker with inspiration and the energy to create. The golden dragons of summer were shown to be much more than keepers of treasure. The dragons of victory encouraged the seeker to celebrate their personal triumphs. The harvest dragons were your partners in gathering what you had planted during this wheel walk.

An Ouroboros—inverted from chapter one

Go and read again the journal entries from this wheel walk. Reflect upon them often with visualizations from your journey. Experience the meditations again and note how each time you sense something new. Continue to record your communions with the dragons. In years to come, I assure you that these writings will become invaluable to your magickal path and practice.

THE WORLD DRAGON AND THE DRAGON SEEKER

Above all, if you have not already done so, recognize and acknowledge your journey as that of the world dragon. Yes, the ouroboros is *YOUR* journey. You help create infinity by knowing. This knowing brings you closer to wholeness. Know and embrace the primal cycle: creation, destruction, and rebirth. Know that the dragon energy is an integral part of the pattern. Know that the dragon and you can become one.

We have explored the lore of many world dragons during this wheel walk. Yet, I assure you, there are many more tales to experience and more sacred sites to discover. In Appendix A, you will find many world dragons with a very brief introduction to their lore and sacred site location. It is my hope that you will continue to seek the dragon energy and experience the magick of dragon lore. May fate smile upon your communions with the dragons!

MEETING THE WORLD DRAGON THROUGH MEDITATION

You have walked the Wheel of the Year in the company of powerful, magickal dragon spirits. You have seen visions of how the dragon energy works with the land to bring balance and wholeness to the world.

Knowing that you are a part of this great cycle, as a partner of the dragon energy, you are ready to meet the spirit of the world dragon.

While in sacred space (or in ritual), clear your mind and let the mundane world's troubles and cares rest aside for this time.

If you are experiencing this meditation alone, record the meditation or have someone you trust read it to you during this communion with the dragons.

Ensure that your surroundings are quiet and that you are completely comfortable (temperature, clothing choice, sitting or lying down, etc.). Make sure that this experience will not be spoiled by mundane annoyances!

Close your eyes and breathe deeply. Allow the cares and concerns of the mundane world to roll away from your neck … your shoulders … your arms … your fingers. Allow your back to relax, from your neck down, down, down, to the base of your spine … and just breathe ….

Allow your focus to rest behind your closed eyes as you feel your body relax completely. You are still. You are quiet.

In your mind's eye, see yourself on a rocky hillside. There are scatterings of dew-moistened grass. The air is clear and fresh. The sun is warm upon your face. The energy of this place, of this time, is solid, good, and strong.

You stand at the bottom slope of a tall, snow-crested mountain. As you look up, you see a path that leads up the mountain.

Begin walking upon the mountain path, slowly, slowly, slowly ascending. Each footstep is deliberate and sure. Your breathing is deep and satisfying.

You have been here before.

Take a few more steps and you will see the runestone. Take the path leading from the stone. Within a few steps, you see the entrance to the Cavern of Crystal, Scales, and Stone.

Herein lies the answer.

Look to the right of the cavern's entrance. There you will find a torch, lantern, or candle. Take the light and step into the cavern.

You will be a light to the World.

As you enter the first chamber, you sense the presence of the guardian dragon. Stop, remove your shoes, and bow. Send a greeting with your name and your purpose for coming to the cavern.

Greetings, Ancient One.
I, [your name], come in peace and love, a humble seeker.
We know you, the dragon replies. You are most welcome here.
Now, the time has come for you to know me.

The cavern brightens with a subtle, golden glow. As your vision adjusts to the light, you see what looks like a wall of golden scales just a few feet in front of where you stand. The scales ripple slowly. Your eyes follow the ripple of energy as it moves clockwise around the cavern. The wall of golden scales continues.

When you have made a complete circle of the cavern, you realize that all around you coils an enormous dragon. Just in front of you, from behind its golden body, the head of a mighty dragon rises.

Do you know me? the dragon asks.

Your thoughts recall the journey that you have made with dragons of the world.

Remember and visualize

the ancient and mighty ones (pause for three breaths)

the ice dragons (pause for three breaths)
the hearth dragons (pause for three breaths)
the waking dragon (pause for three breaths)
the dragons of making (pause for three breaths)
the golden dragons of summer (pause for three breaths)
the dragons of victory (pause for three breaths)
the harvest dragons (pause for three breaths)

Even as you visualize all of these dragons, you sense that *this* dragon is something quite different. It is familiar to you ... you've felt this energy before ....

I am the world dragon.
I am wholeness.
I am completeness.
I am infinity.
I am the journey's beginning.
I am the journey's end.

Bow low as you stand before Jormungandr, the world serpent.

Behold, the world dragon says.

The cavern becomes even brighter. You can clearly see the beautiful ouroboros fully encircling the cavern. Upon the walls of the cavern, you see drawings of dragons interacting with humans. It seems to be a story ....

In the north, you see a young man sitting by a fire. Above his image, atop a hoard of gold, lies Fafnir of the ice and snow. (Pause for three breaths.)

In the northeast, you see a great dragon encircling a house. The dragon is at rest, with one eye closed, but the other eye is wide and watching. It is the guardian of the home. (Pause for three breaths.)

In the east, you see a dragon sitting next to a human. Their mouths are open as if in song, and their faces, dragon and human, are full of joy and life. (Pause for three breaths.)

In the southeast, you see a river flowing and above it, in it, and within it, a dragon sits as guardian, ever watchful and aware. (Pause for three breaths.)

In the south, a dragon and human, the same human from the east drawing, again sit together. They also appear to be singing. (Pause for three breaths.)

In the southwest, two dragons, white and red, battle above a rocky hilltop. (Pause for three breaths.)

In the west, a dragon and many humans are harvesting crops from a field. (Pause for three breaths.)

This is your journey, says the world serpent.

Thank the world serpent for this journey.

Take some time to linger in the cavern and explore the drawings. Speak to the world serpent, if you wish.

The journey is over
And now it begins anew.

Take three deep breaths. Concentrate upon the back of your closed eyes. With your next breath, you feel a shift in the energy around you. You begin to feel a bit heavier as you become aware of your body.

You have returned to your safe and sacred space in this world. You feel refreshed by this communion with the dragons.

Now, one more deep breath … and open your eyes.

APPENDIX A

MAGICKAL DRAGONS

As you continue your work with dragon energy, you will, no doubt, encounter other dragons. This appendix includes the dragons discussed in this book as well as other archetypal dragons. Each of these archetypes has a very specific energy and color. While this appendix does attempt to act as a guide for identifying dragon energies, it is in no way a complete listing of magickal dragons. Continue your journey and add to this appendix with your own research of dragon lore and dragon sacred sites.

ALBANIA

Bolla, Battle Dragon
The Bolla is a female serpent who, if she remains unseen by humans, will evolve into a formidable dragon known as a *kulshedra*. It was most likely a kulshedra in the tales of Saint George and the dragon (see chapter five).

Blue Eye, Water Dragon
A dragon that emerged from the sea and brought chaos and strife to the land and people of Albania. While in great pain, the Blue Eye serpent wept until one of its eyes fell out and formed a deep spring (see chapter five).

Dragua, Battle Dragon

A dragua is a male Albanian dragon. The dragua is the true "enemy" of the kulshedra (see chapter five).

BABYLON (MODERN-DAY IRAQ)
Tiamat, Ancient and Mighty Primordial Creation Dragon

One of the most ancient of dragons. Tiamat appeared as both human and dragon. She is one of the Annunaki, the old gods, and is called *Ummu-Hubur*, "she who formed all things" (see chapter two).

Mushhushshu-dragon, Ancient and Mighty Guardian of Gods

The Mushhushshu-dragon is also known as the "dragon of Marduk." This ancient dragon is a creature with scales covering its body, a serpentine head with viper horns, the front feet of a cat, the hind legs of a bird, and a tail much like a scorpion's (see chapter two).

Illuyankas, Ancient and Mighty Chaos Dragon

In the ancient world of the Hittites, the storm god, Taru, and the dragon, Illuyankas, were mortal enemies. Their battle was reenacted every spring by the Hittites as part of *puruli*, their spring festival (see chapter two).

Kur, Ancient and Mighty Guardian Dragon of the Underworld

The Sumerian dragon, Kur, is a dense, thick manifestation of energy that is a guardian of the underworld. The lore from the Enki and Kur tale is perhaps the oldest dragon slaying story (see chapter two).

CANAAN (MODERN-DAY ISRAEL, GAZA STRIP, AND WEST BANK)
Yam: Nahar, Ancient and Mighty Primordial Chaos Dragon

Yam-Nahar is primordial destruction (and creation); he is a sea dragon with power that is untamed and raging (see chapter two).

EGYPT

Apep, Ancient and Mighty Chaos Dragon and World Dragon

Enemy of Ra, Lord of Chaos, the cyclic adversary of the solar deity, Ra. Apep and Ra battle daily, and through this confrontation, the world is kept in balance. Apep's ability to be anywhere and everywhere earned him the additional title of *World Encircler.* Egyptian ouroboros (see chapter two).

Mehen, Ancient and Mighty Guardian of Gods

Every day as Ra travels the sky, the dragon, Mehen, coils around the god's sun boat and guards against any threat to Ra's task. *Mehen* actually means "coiled one" in Egyptian (see chapter two).

CHINA

There are over one hundred ancient dragon names mentioned in Chinese texts. Here is a small sampling of those named dragons.

Tianlong, Prime Mover

A celestial dragon that guards heavenly palaces and pulls divine chariots; the Chinese name for the constellation most often called Draco.

Shenlong, Elemental Dragon

A thunder dragon that controls the weather.

Dilong, Elemental Dragon

A controller of rivers and seas.

GREECE

Typhon, Ancient and Mighty Fire Dragon

Typhon is the youngest son of Gaia and Tarturus. He has a hundred dragon heads and is a formidable, even monstrous, force. His energy is closely associated with volcanoes and especially their eruptions. His offspring include the Hydra, the Chimera, and sometimes, Ladon.

Ladon: Guardian of Sacred Site and Object

Like many of the Greek dragons, Ladon is born during the age of the Titans. His parentage depends upon whom you ask, but more often than not, his mother is Gaia.

Ladon is a sentinel and guardian dragon for the Golden Apples that are kept in the Garden of the Hesperides. Herakles is tasked with stealing these apples; which, of course, requires that this dragon either be coaxed to surrender them or be slain. Herakles, in most versions, kills Ladon. The very next day after Herakles has taken the apples, Jason and the Argonauts pass near the Garden and hear the cries of the Hesperides as they weep over the twitching corpse of the dragon.

Lernaean Hydra: Guardian to the Underworld

Sometimes simply called "the Hydra," this creature is the offspring of Typhon and Echidna. This is a guardian dragon for an entrance to the Underworld. His breath is so venomous that just one breath could kill a grown man. His blood, too, contains deadly venom, and he has many heads (the lore differs on exactly how many). If one of his heads is lost, two grow in its place.

The second labor of Herakles required the hero to slay the Hydra. In fact, Hera, the wife of Zeus, had been planning this encounter for quite some time: she had raised the Hydra with the explicit intent of killing Herakles.

Herakles struggles to overcome this powerful dragon; it is finally with fire (and the assistance of his nephew, Iolaus) that the hero manages to stop the dragon from reproducing heads. Herakles defeats the Hydra and takes some of the venomous blood to use as a weapon for his future enemies.

The Hydra was said to dwell near the Lerna region of ancient Greece. This area had many springs, some marshes, and a lake. Its location is believed to be on the east coast of the Peloponnesus in southern Greece, just south of Argos.

Pytho, Guardian of Sacred Site and Object

Pytho is the Greek dragon who dwelled at the "center of the world," Delphi, Greece. Pytho, sometimes called Pythos or Python, guarded the omphalos for the cult of Gaia until Apollo slew him (see chapter nine).

Colchian, Guardian of Sacred Site and Object

This dragon dwelled in the grove of Ares in the ancient kingdom of Colchis, Greece. We know Colchis as modern-day Georgia, a coastal country on the Black Sea. This dragon was the sacred guardian of the Golden Fleece, which was a ram's skin much loved by Zeus. The dragon was enormous and was said to never sleep (see chapter seven).

Medea's Dragons, Prime Mover Dragons

These dragons are quite different from guardian dragons. Images upon vases and urns depict them as a pair of enormous serpents that coil and encircle the entire chariot. The dragons do not have wings in the ancient drawings, but several writings of Medea's tale specifically state that these dragons were indeed winged "drakones."[20]

Draco

The constellation Draco has been recognized and catalogued by many cultures. To the Greeks, the constellation was formed as an homage to the great battle between Herakles and Ladon. For the Romans, it was Minerva (Greek Athena) who defeated the dragon and then tossed it to the stars where it formed into the Draco arrangement.

SCANDINAVIA

Beowulf's Dragon, Guardian Dragon

A nameless dragon and mighty hoard-keeper known from the famous Anglo-Saxon poem, *Beowulf*.

Fafnir, Guardian Dragon

Fafnir was a mighty guardian of a vast treasure of gold and jewels. He was an evolved creature in that he was a human before his greed transformed him. His story can be found on runestones all over Scandinavia (see chapter three).

---

20. Ovid, *Metamorphoses*, 23.

WALES

The Red Dragon of Britain, Battle Dragon

The red dragon is one of the "sleeping" dragons of Dinas Emrys. This dragon was the manifestation of the land of Britain in the time of Vortigern. As Vortigern tried to build his fortress, each night the red dragon would wake and engage in battle with the white Saxon dragon. The dragon battles would destroy any progress that had been made by Vortigern's engineers (see chapter eight).

The White Saxon Dragon, Battle Dragon

Famous from the prophecies of Merlin, the white Saxon dragon rested beneath the Iron Age hillfort named Dinas Emrys. Legend says that the Saxon dragon battled every night with a red dragon, the dragon of Britain, (see chapter eight).

DRAGONS FROM MODERN LITERATURE

Unlike the ancient lore, these tales do not belong to any single culture; instead, these dragons belong to us, modern humans. Although the lore of these dragons is not ancient, their tales have affected modern culture on a global scale. This is a small sampling of dragons in twentieth and twenty-first century literature. There are many, many more to explore!

Ancalagon the Black, Battle Dragon: Dragon of Victory
(from J. R. R. Tolkien's *The Silmarillion*)

Ancalagon is a flightless but fire-breathing dragon created by the Dark Lord Morgoth during the First Age of Middle Earth. He is a winged dragon who fought in the wars between Morgoth and the Elves and Men. Not quite a god, Ancalagon is a Maiar, a very powerful spirit residing in physical form. He is an evil and cunning dragon capable of human speech. This dragon energy is dark, heavy, and fierce. The seeker is warned not to approach this dragon energy directly.

Chrysophylax Dives, Guardian Dragon: Harvest Dragon
(from J. R. R. Tolkien's *Farmer Giles of Ham*)

Chrysophylax Dives is a dragon who is almost fearless. He is cunning, greedy, and formidable. Yet, he also acts as the catalyst for Farmer Giles to ascend in life well beyond his wildest dreams. Chrysophylax Dives was capable of human speech. This dragon energy is wily and intimidating, but upon closer inspection, his reluctance to fight will be sensed. The seeker is cautioned to approach this dragon energy with caution.

Drogon, Battle and Guardian Dragon: Hearth Dragon
(from George R. R. Martin's A Song of Ice and Fire series)

The largest of three dragon siblings, Drogon is a winged and fire-breathing protector of his queen and Mother of Dragons, Daenerys Targaryen. Drogon is raised by Daenerys and takes her into battle on several occasions. Drogon understood his "mother" and the actions of humans, but he was not capable of human speech. This dragon energy is heavy, protective, and vast. The seeker should be cautious in approaching this dragon energy.

Glaurung the Golden, Battle Dragon: Golden Dragon of Summer
(from J. R. R. Tolkien's *The Silmarillion*)

A flightless but fire-breathing terror, Glaurung was the first and perhaps the most fearsome of the Dark Lord Morgoth's dragon creations. At the bidding of Morgoth, Glaurung used his power and his twisted words to make the life of the human, Turin Turambar, a life of woe. This dragon was capable of human speech and is also called Glaurung the Evil and Glaurung the Deceiver. This dragon energy is hot, intense, and frightening. The seeker is warned not to approach this dragon energy directly.

Rhaegal, Battle and Guardian Dragon: Hearth Dragon
(from George R. R. Martin's A Song of Ice and Fire series)

One of three dragon siblings, Rhaegal is a winged, fire-breathing battle dragon. Like his brothers Drogon and Viserion, Rhaegal is a protector of the Mother of Dragons, Daenerys Targaryen. Rhaegal was not capable of human speech.

This dragon energy is lean and airy. The seeker should be cautious in approaching this dragon energy.

Scatha the Worm, Guardian Dragon: Ancestor Dragon
(from J. R. R. Tolkien's The Lord of the Rings)

Scatha was a dragon who possessed a great hoard of jewels and gold. Both the Dwarves and the Men of Eotheod claimed the right to the treasure. Not unlike many Norse tales, the conflicts that arise because of this contested treasure are tragic and many. Scatha was wingless and probably fire-breathing. The seeker is warned not to approach this dragon energy directly.

Smaug the Golden, Guardian Dragon: Harvest Dragon
(from J. R. R. Tolkien's The Hobbit)

Smaug was a fire-breathing dragon who stole the vast riches and kingdom from the Dwarves of Erebor. Smaug was the supposed last dragon in Middle Earth during the Third Age. Smaug was capable of human speech. This dragon energy is scalding hot and will feel very close. The seeker is warned not to approach this dragon energy directly.

Viserion, Guardian Dragon: Hearth Dragon ~ Ice Dragon
(from George R. R. Martin's A Song of Ice and Fire series and
Game of Thrones)

One of three dragon siblings, Viserion is a winged, fire-breathing battle dragon. For most of his life, Viserion is a protector of the Mother of Dragons, Daenerys Targaryen. In the television adaptation, Game of Thrones, he is transformed into an ice dragon. Rhaegal was not capable of human speech. This dragon energy is cold and deep. The seeker should be cautious in approaching this dragon energy.

Saphira, Battle and Guardian Dragon: Harvest Dragon
(from Christopher Paolini's The Inheritance Cycle)

Saphira is found as an egg by a young farm boy named Eragon who has no idea what he has found. She hatches after the boy cares for her, and together, they become a formidable battle dragon and dragon rider duo. Saphira is winged and is capable of human speech. Her bond with humans, especially her rider, is strong. Saphira's dragon energy is cool and strong. The seeker should approach this dragon energy with respect.

Toothless, Battle and Guardian Dragon: Victory Dragon
(from Cressida Cowell's How to Train Your Dragon series)

Toothless is a winged dragon that is known as a Night Fury dragon in this world; he becomes bonded with a young Viking boy who eventually becomes the dragon's rider and battle companion. Together, the dragon and Viking boy end the war between the Vikings and the dragons. Toothless does not speak "human" speech, but he is able to communicate with humans through gesture and movement. This dragon energy is dark, wispy, and fierce. However, to his allies and bonded friends, his loyalty has no limits. The seeker should approach this dragon energy with respect.

Falcor, Prime Mover Dragon: Harvest Dragon
(from Michael Ende's *The Neverending Story*)

Falcor is a white, winged dragon who acts as a "mover between worlds" for the two boy heroes of our world and the world of *The Neverending Story*. Falcor is able to move between worlds and carry heroes to their destinies. He is capable of human speech. His energy is cool, strong, and airy. The seeker should approach this dragon energy with respect.

Norbert, Battle and Guardian Dragon: Victory Dragon
(from J. K. Rowling's Harry Potter series)

Norbert is a fire-breathing and winged Norwegian Ridgeback dragon from the world of Harry Potter. Norbert is hatched and adopted by a kind animal keeper named Rubeus Hagrid. Norbert turns out to be a female dragon and quite vicious. Her name is changed to Norberta and Romania becomes her new home. This dragon energy is vicious and lean. The seeker is warned not to approach this dragon energy directly.

BIBLIOGRAPHY

"Albanian Legend: How Was the 'Blue Eye' Water Spring Created?" Invest in Albania. July 9, 2015. https://invest-in-albania.org/albanian-legend-how -was-the-blue-eye-water-spring-created/.

Amen, Ra Un Nefer. *Metu Neter, vol. 1: The Great Oracle of Tehuti and the Egyptian system of Spiritual Cultivation.* New York: Kamit Publications, 1990.

Apollonius of Rhodes. *Jason and the Argonauts.* New York: Penguin Classics, 2014.

Base, Graeme. *The Discovery of Dragons.* New York: Harry N. Abrams, 1996.

Campbell, J. F. *The Celtic Dragon Myth: With the Geste of Fraoch and the Dragon.* New York: David De Angelis, 2017.

Faulkner, Raymond O. "The Bremner-Rhind Papyrus: III: D. The Book of Overthrowing 'Apep" *The Journal of Egyptian Archaeology* 23, no. 2 (December 1937): 166–185. https://www.jstor.org/stable/3854422.

Gruffydd, William John. *Folklore and Myth in the Mabinogion: A Lecture Delivered at the National Museum of Wales on 27 October 1950.* New York: Read Books, 2013.

"Hattusha: The Hittite Capital," World Heritage List, UNESCO World Heritage, accessed May 14, 2020. https://whc.unesco.org/en/list/377/.

Henes, Mama Donna. *Bless this House: Creating Sacred Space Where You Live, Work & Travel.* New York: Ixia Press, 2018.

Jordan, Michael. *Dictionary of Gods and Goddesses.* New York: Facts on File, 1993.

Lurker, Manfred. *The Routledge Dictionary of Gods and Goddesses, Devils and Demons.* New York: Routledge, 2004.

McCaffrey, Anne. *A Diversity of Dragons.* With Richard Woods. New York: Harper Voyager, 1997.

McCullough, Joseph A. *Dragonslayers: From Beowulf to St. George.* New York: Osprey Publishing, 2013.

"Monastery of St. Nicolas," St. Nicholas Center, accessed May 15, 2020. https://www.stnicholascenter.org/gazetteer/2929.

Morris, Tisha. *Decorating with the Five Elements of Feng Shui.* Woodbury, MN: Llewellyn Publications, 2015.

Niles, Doug. *Dragons: The Myths, Legends, & Lore.* New York: Simon and Schuster, 2013.

Ovid. *Metamorphoses.* New York: Penguin Classics, 2004.

"St. Nicholas (Mesopotam) Monastery," Into Albania, accessed May 15, 2020. https://www.intoalbania.com/attraction/st-nicholas-mesopotam-monastery/.

Stephens, George. *Prof. S. Bugge's Studies on Northern Mythology Shortly Examined.* London: Williams and Norgate, 1883.

The Saga of the Volsungs. Digireads, 2005.

Tolkien, J. R. R. *The Legend of Sigurd and Gudrún.* New York: Mariner Books, 2010.

Waggoner, Ben, trans. *The Sagas of Ragnar Lodbrok.* Chicago: The Troth Publications, 2018.

Wallis Budge, E. A. *The Gods of the Egyptians: Or Studies in Egyptian Mythology.* Vol. 1, *Studies in Egyptian Mythology in Two Volumes.* New York: Dover Publications: 1969.

Wilkinson, Richard H. *The Complete Gods and Goddesses of Ancient Egypt.* London: Thames & Hudson, 2017.

RECOMMENDED READING

In addition to the specific titles listed below, there are certain authors whose work I particularly recommend: All books by Caitlin and John Matthews, Delores Ashcroft-Nowicki, R. J. Stewart, Gareth Knight, Joseph Campbell, Kahlil Gibran, and Dion Fortune.

Greco-Roman Myth and Lore

Metamorphosis, Ovid
The Greek Myths, Robert Graves
Myths of Greece and Rome, Thomas Bullfinch

Celtic Myth and Lore

The Mabinogion, Lady Charlotte Guest
Encyclopedia of Celtic Wisdom, Caitlin and John Matthews

Egyptian Myth and Lore

The Egyptian Book of the Dead, available in various translations
Gods of Ancient Egypt, Barbara Watterson

Feng Shui

Decorating with the Five Elements of Feng Shui, Tisha Morris

General Magick
The Ritual Magick Workbook, Delores Ashcroft-Nowicki
Living Magical Arts, R. J. Stewart
Advanced Magical Arts, R. J. Stewart

Ritual
The Psychology of Ritual, Murray Hope

Runes
Taking Up the Runes: A Complete Guide to Using Runes in Spells, Divination, and Magic, Diana Paxson
The Runes, Freya Aswynn

Sound and Sonics
The Spiritual Dimension of Music, R. J. Stewart
Music and the Elemental Psyche, R. J. Stewart
Singing the Soul Back Home, Caitlin Matthews

Wheel of the Year
Eight Sabbats for Witches, Janet and Stewart Farrar
Wheel of the Year and Rites of Passage, Paula Campanelli

TO WRITE TO THE AUTHOR

If you wish to contact the author or would like more information about this book, please write to the author in care of Llewellyn Worldwide Ltd. and we will forward your request. Both the author and publisher appreciate hearing from you and learning of your enjoyment of this book and how it has helped you. Llewellyn Worldwide Ltd. cannot guarantee that every letter written to the author can be answered, but all will be forwarded. Please write to:

Virginia Chandler
℅ Llewellyn Worldwide
2143 Wooddale Drive
Woodbury, MN 55125-2989
Please enclose a self-addressed stamped envelope for reply,
or $1.00 to cover costs. If outside the U.S.A., enclose
an international postal reply coupon.

Many of Llewellyn's authors have websites with additional information and resources. For more information, please visit our website at http://www.llewellyn.com